THE SUCCESS ALGORITHM

Unleashing Your Full Potential in The Software World

SREENATH NATARAJAN

ISBN
Hardcase 979-8-89724-510-9
Paperback 979-8-89699-3 79-7

Dedication

This book is wholeheartedly dedicated to all software professionals, irrespective of experience or role, to every aspiring engineer, passionate trainer, and visionary freelancer, and to everyone who is deeply engaged in the art and science of software.

Contents

Foreword.. 7

Acknowledgement 9

Motivation for Writing This Book................................ 11

Why You Need to Read This Book................................. 13

Author's Legal and Ethical Statement........................... 15

Decoding the Success Algorithm 16

Chapter 1:   Code Your Mindset: Diagnosing Current Limitations......... 27

Chapter 2:   Refactoring Your Thinking: Upgrading to a
Growth Mindset 43

Chapter 3:   Agile Goal Setting: Navigating Your Software Career.......... 54

Chapter 4:   Debugging Challenges: Cultivating Resilience 66

Chapter 5:   The Web of Opportunity: Interlacing Connections
for Career Advancement 86

Chapter 6:   The Learning River: Flowing with Change in the
Tech Landscape 106

Chapter 7:   The Human Circuit: Powering Tech Teams with
Emotional Intelligence... 115

Chapter 8:   Visionary Coding: Crafting Your Career Path 135

Contents

Chapter 9: Planting Seeds of Innovation: Cultivating Creativity and Problem-Solving Skills for Growth 149

Chapter 10: Building the Bridge to Success: Tracking Milestones and Metrics 169

Chapter 11: Harvesting the Fruits of Success: The Role of Recognition in the Software World 180

Chapter 12: Navigating Career Transitions and Growth Opportunities 185

Chapter 13: The Ritual Algorithm: Programming Success into Your Life 202

Your Journey Ahead: Putting It All Together 217

The Concluding Message of the Success Algorithm 220

Summary of Key Revisions 221

References and Further Reading 223

Disclaimer 233

About Author 235

Foreword

Success in the fast-paced software industry can feel like a complex algorithm—challenging to decode and even harder to master. *The Success Algorithm: Unleashing Your Full Potential in the Software World* by Sreenath Natarajan is a practical and empowering guide for anyone looking to optimise their mindset and achieve meaningful career growth in this dynamic field.

As a Mind Performance Coach and author of *Unleash the Power of Reading,* I have seen how cultivating the right mindset can transform not only careers but lives. Sreenaths's book highlights this beautifully, focusing on the importance of overcoming self-doubt, embracing resilience, and fostering continuous learning—all crucial for thriving in the software industry.

This book is more than just a professional guide—it's a tool for personal transformation. By addressing both the technical and emotional challenges of a career in tech, it bridges the gap between professional excellence and personal fulfilment. Readers will learn how to align their values with their goals, creating a sense of purpose and direction that drives long-term success.

What sets this book apart is its holistic approach. From setting impactful goals to building emotional intelligence and leveraging feedback, it provides actionable strategies to help software professionals at any career stage achieve clarity, confidence, and lasting success. With real-world examples and practical tools, Natarajan ensures readers can immediately apply these insights to create a meaningful and fulfilling career.

Whether you're just starting out or looking to elevate your tech career, *The Success Algorithm* will inspire and empower you to unlock your full potential.

Best wishes,

(Dr. Manjunath M.S.)
Mind Performance Coach and Author of "Unleash the Power of Reading"

Acknowledgement

I am deeply grateful to all those who have supported, guided, and inspired me throughout this journey.

First and foremost, I dedicate this book to Lord Krishna, my lord, guru, enlightener, and invisible friend. His wisdom and guidance have been an unwavering source of strength and inspiration, illuminating my path with clarity and purpose.

To my beloved family—your unwavering love and strength have been my greatest source of inspiration.

I am deeply grateful to Dr. Manjunath, my guru and mentor, whose profound psychological insights not only transformed my perspective but also ignited the spark within me to write this book. Your wisdom has been a guiding light, and I carry it with me every step of this journey.

A special thank you to Mona Sheeba D, my CBL colleague and successful software professional, whose invaluable suggestions have greatly enriched this book.

I extend my sincere appreciation to my learning friends and facilitators for their invaluable suggestions and guidance, which have further enriched this work.

To all my present and past managers, mentors, colleagues, and friends, thank you for your wisdom and support, which have profoundly shaped my professional journey. Your contributions have left an indelible mark on my life.

To my teachers, lecturers and friends, your efforts laid the foundation of my educational path and nurtured my intellectual curiosity.

Finally, to every person who has been part of this journey—your love, encouragement, and guidance have made this book a reality. Thank you, one and all.

Motivation for Writing This Book

I didn't write this book just to talk about success.

I wrote it because I've felt the **silent struggles** that so many software professionals carry behind their screens.

The pressure to constantly prove yourself.
The burnout masked as productivity.
The fear of falling behind in a world that never slows down.
The quiet voice inside that says, *"Am I enough?"*

I've seen brilliant minds doubt themselves, tireless professionals lose direction, and passionate coders feel disconnected from the very work they once loved. I've been there too. And what I realized is this:

We don't just need better tools. We need better thinking. We need healing. We need purpose.

The Success Algorithm was born from a desire to **reignite the human spirit within the technical world**—to help you not just survive the tech industry, but truly **thrive** in it.

This book is my heart speaking to yours. It's a collection of everything I've learned through my own battles—self-doubt, setbacks, reinvention, and rediscovery. It's for the quiet professionals who give so much, but rarely pause to nourish their own growth. It's for the dreamers, the late-night coders, the mid-career wanderers, the ones questioning where they truly belong.

I wrote this book to remind you that:

- **You are not alone.**

- **You are not stuck.**

- **And you are more than your job title, your code, or your current role.**

There is a power within you that no algorithm can replicate.

A potential that no circumstance can limit.

And a success story that only *you* can write.

If this book helps even one person break free from burnout, rediscover their confidence, or find peace in the midst of pressure—then every word will have been worth it.

This is not just a guide. It's a light.

And I hope it helps you see yourself—and your path—more clearly than ever before.

– Sreenath Natarajan

Why You Need to Read This Book

In the tech industry, you're taught to master tools, frameworks, and deadlines—

But **no one teaches you how to master yourself.**

You may be doing all the right things on paper—upskilling, working hard, staying committed—

Yet deep inside, you may feel stuck, overlooked, or unsure of your next move.

Why?

Because success isn't just about what you know.

It's about how you *think*, how you *grow*, and how you *break through your own mental limits*.

The Success Algorithm is a transformational guide for software professionals who are ready to:

- Break free from **self-doubt, fear, and imposter syndrome**

- Cultivate a mindset of **continuous learning and unstoppable growth**

- Build meaningful, value-driven **networks and relationships**

- Use **emotional intelligence** to navigate stress, change, and complexity

- Align your career path with **your purpose and passion**

- Develop clarity, confidence, and inner drive—without chasing superficial success

This book isn't filled with fluff or generic advice. It's built on real-world experience—battle-tested lessons from someone who's lived the journey, faced the struggles, and found the mindset that unlocks true growth.

If you've ever:

- Felt left behind in a fast-moving industry

- Hit a wall despite working hard

- Questioned your self-worth or future in tech

- Dreamed of becoming your best self, but didn't know how…

Then *The Success Algorithm* will speak to your core.

This is your guide to **overcoming internal roadblocks**, embracing lifelong learning, and creating a career you don't just survive in—but thrive in.

Because the real breakthrough doesn't come from outside.

It starts from *within*.

Let *The Success Algorithm* help you rewrite the code of your career—and your life.

Author's Legal and Ethical Statement

I, the author, affirm that this book, *The Success Algorithm: Unleashing Your Full Potential in the Software World*, is an original work based on my personal experiences, research, and reflections in the software industry. Where external ideas, concepts, or references are incorporated, proper credit has been given to the best of my knowledge.

This book is intended solely for educational, motivational, and informational purposes. It does not provide professional legal, financial, medical, or career advice. I recommend readers seek advice from qualified professionals to address their unique situations.

All trademarks, product names, and platform references mentioned are the property of their respective owners and are used for illustrative purposes only. Case studies and scenarios have been anonymised or fictionalised to protect individual privacy.

While every effort has been made to ensure accuracy and originality, the author welcomes corrections and acknowledgements in future editions. The author and publisher are not liable for any consequences stemming from the application of information contained in this work.

By reading this book, the reader acknowledges that they are solely responsible for their interpretation and use of the material presented.

Decoding the Success Algorithm

Welcome! You're about to begin a journey that could redefine your career.

Are you seeking clarity, growth, and lasting impact in your professional life? Then you've found the right book.

If you think the **Success Algorithm** is just a concept, it's more than that. It's a **mindset**, a **strategy**, and a **roadmap** for achieving meaningful success.

But what exactly is it? Let's start by breaking down the two powerful words: **Success** and **Algorithm**.

The definition of **success** varies from person to person, and it evolves.

For a bookshop owner, success might mean selling the highest number of books in a given period. For a farmer, it could be overcoming nature's challenges to produce a bountiful crop. For a teacher, success may lie in helping students deeply understand a subject or scaling their knowledge to reach more learners or to learn new, creative teaching methods.

In the tech world, it's just as diverse.

A developer might define success as shipping a clean, impactful feature.

A manager might focus on building and leading high-performing teams.

A Vice President might measure success through strategic growth, innovation, long-term business outcomes and so on.

Whatever the role, **success keeps evolving**. It's never a "one-and-done" goal. It's a **journey**, as thought leaders like Zig Ziglar, Arthur Ashe, and Earl Nightingale have wisely emphasised.

Once a developer completes a successful feature, what's next? Is that the end of success?

Of course not—because success is **redefined at every level**.

This idea has echoed through time:

- Zig Ziglar said success is something we walk toward every day (*See You at the Top*, 1975).

- Arthur Ashe reminded us, "Success is a journey, not a destination..."

- Earl Nightingale described success as "the progressive realisation of a worthy ideal" (*The Strangest Secret*, 1956).

In other words, **success is a moving target**—and that's what makes it meaningful.

Let's distil this further for software professionals to make it easier for this book:

Success isn't just about job titles, salaries, or project milestones. It's about **evolving with purpose, solving meaningful problems**, and **growing with every sprint, every commit, and every conversation.**

Think of it like crafting a complex algorithm—your career unfolds line by line, shaped by intention and persistence.

Understanding Algorithm

Now let's explore the second part of the phrase: **Algorithm**.

If you come from a computer science background, this term is already familiar. But I say "or" because many professionals change domains after graduation or shift paths during their careers.

Let me explain it with a simple, real-life analogy: **cooking.**

Before preparing a meal, I:

- Assess the available ingredients

- Gather what I need

- Wash, peel, and prep them

- Cook in a specific order

- Let the dish rest, and serve it

That's an **algorithm**—a step-by-step process to reach a desired outcome.

If I skip a step or do things in the wrong order, the dish may turn out poorly.

Similarly, your **career success** depends on following a deliberate, evolving process—an **algorithm** shaped by mindset, action, and adaptability.

The Success Algorithm

So, what is the **Success Algorithm**?

The Success Algorithm is a methodical, step-by-step approach to solving meaningful problems, evolving with purpose, and continuously improving toward personal and professional fulfilment.

In the software field, it's about more than just writing clean code or managing projects.

It's about systematically identifying valuable problems, approaching them with clarity, and constantly improving across every dimension of your career.

It's not just technical or leadership skills—it's your overall **attitude toward growth**, or what psychologist **Dr. Carol Dweck** calls your **mindset**—something we'll explore in the next section.

Why Is Embracing Growth Essential?

Let's take the example of a software developer, **Sumukh**.

He was brilliant. In the beginning, he excelled in his job. Everything seemed perfect, and life was going smoothly. He was enjoying his job!

But as technology progressed, his company began transitioning to modern architectures and cutting-edge platforms.

Sumukh, however, **resisted change**. May be because of procrastination. He continued using outdated tools and methods, without upgrading himself or learning new skills.

Was that the right choice?

Then came a turning point. One day, the project where he had long excelled finally came to an end. The company now expects its employees to be equipped with up-to-date skills to move to new, high-impact projects.

Unfortunately, **Sumukh couldn't fit into any of them**.

His brilliance no longer mattered because he had not evolved.

In the tech world, **standing still is the fastest way to fall behind**.

Eventually, Sumukh was no longer the go-to person in the team and the entire group.

He became the **last choice**. Hurts? But it's a fact!!

Sumukh's story is a powerful reminder:

In today's fast-paced digital world, **adaptability and continuous learning are not optional—they are essential.**

Understanding the concept of mindset and its categories.

Have you ever wondered why some people achieve so much in life while others struggle, even when they seem equally talented? Why is it that in the same environment—even in the IT field—one person climbs the ladder effortlessly while another keeps hitting walls? Is it all about intelligence? Or talent? Not really.

Some believe that **hard work** makes the difference, while others point to **natural ability**. But what separates those who move forward from those who stay stuck?

In one simple word—it's **mindset**.

A renowned psychologist, **Dr. Carol Dweck**, transformed the way we understand success. Through her ground breaking research, she introduced the concept of **"mindset"**, which communicates that success isn't just about talent or intelligence—it's about how we **approach growth and learning**.

It's the difference between believing you're either born with the ability or that you can build it. That belief alone shapes how you face challenges, bounce back from setbacks, and ultimately create your path to success.

Dr. Carol Dweck, through her experiments, found that people generally fall into two realms when it comes to how they view their abilities: **fixed-mindset** and **growth-mindset** individuals.

Fixed-mindset people believe their capabilities are limited and that intelligence is something you're born with, not something you can develop. They often think that talent is static, and because of this belief, they shy away from challenges, avoid effort, and stay in their comfort zones. This mindset holds them back from reaching their true potential.

They tend to give up easily when things get tough, and failures hit them hard. Sometimes, they even feel threatened by other people's success.

You'll often hear this mindset in action through statements like:

"I can't handle this project anymore. Such things are not for me."
"I don't think I can fix this bug"
"I'm afraid that this task might consume my time."
"How can I survive if lost the job!!"

These beliefs don't reflect actual limitations—they reflect the walls created by a fixed mindset.

But there's another way to look at challenges—and life. Embrace the **growth mindset.**

With **a growth mindset**, one can develop abilities over time through effort, learning, and persistence. They understand that setbacks are not signs of failure, but stepping stones toward improvement. Instead of avoiding difficulty, they embrace it—because they see every challenge as a chance to grow.

They **don't** say, *"I can't do this."*
They **say**, *"I can't do this yet—but I can learn."*

This mindset empowers people to stay resilient in the face of failure, to value feedback instead of fearing it, and to find inspiration in the success of others rather than feeling threatened by it.

You'll often hear growth-minded individuals say things like:

"Let me try a different approach."
"This isn't working yet, but I'll figure it out."
"I'm handling conflicts for the first time. I may not be perfect, but I'm confident I can learn and manage them with grace."
"I always look for new opportunities"

In the fast-changing modern world, this mindset isn't just a choice - it's a must. Embracing a growth mindset allows you to achieve your goals.

So decide which mindset you want to have!!

The Success Algorithm in Software World

We have already seen the definition of "The Success Algorithm". Now Let's go deeper further. The computer algorithm becomes the heart of any software product. Software developers often use different algorithms to develop or architect new products or to solve complex issues. The *success algorithm* in the software field is not only limited to technical skills but also associated with crucial soft skills like thinking, attitude towards work, resilience to circumstances, coping with changes and continuous learning that will help you achieve your long-term goals. Designing the correct algorithm is vital for any program to execute efficiently; similarly, developing the right mindset is essential for massive growth in the software industry.

Here are some of the critical components of the success algorithm:

Problem Tackling Approach

In the software field, every individual, from junior engineers to Chief Executive Officers (CEOs), is involved in problem-solving. Problems can occur in different ways depending on the occasion.

It varies on the individual to handle problems. People with a fixed mindset resist complex issues. In contrast, people with a growth mindset demonstrate a success algorithm, wherein they consider complex problems as opportunities for growth and embrace them open-mindedly. The professional who is involved in tackling the issue understands the difficulties, analyses situations, understands requirements, comes up with step-by-step approaches, and executes the approaches.

Resilience

Like organisations, failures are common for individuals at every level. It may involve reopening bugs, addressing feature failures, resolving outages at customer sites, or not getting opportunities to grow, similarly, for all other roles. The most important thing is how to develop resilience. We will discuss strategies to build resilience in Chapter 5: **Debugging Challenges: Cultivating Resilience.**

Adaptability

In the software field, change is constant. Innovations and technologies evolve daily and are reflected in products as well. So, every professional needs to upgrade according to modern trends. We will discuss more about adoptability in Chapter 2: **Refactoring Your Thinking: Upgrading to a Growth Mindset.**

Teamwork and Collaboration

Most software professionals work in a team(s) or group(s), and teamwork and collaboration are required irrespective of their positions or experience level. People with growth mindsets are open to communication, sharing thoughts or ideas, and encouraging themselves to learn from others. In contrast, people with fixed mindsets feel they do not need to open up as they already know things. Sometimes, they refuse to admit it even if they don't know.

Continuous Learning

When a software professional stop learning, he steers towards his career decline. Continuous learning should be a mantra of any software professional, irrespective of position, organization, country, or place. We can compare technologies like a river. Most of the time, new technologies supersede old ones, which has become an ongoing process in the last few decades. With revolutions in the cloud and artificial Intelligence, the trends will continue for a few more decades.

A professional with a dynamic mindset exhibits continuous learning. Technology advances rapidly and evolves practices; these people continuously put effort into staying current regarding their skills.

Resources and strategies: We will discuss more on various strategies for continuous learning in Chapter 7: The Learning River: Flowing with Change in the Tech Landscape

Seeking regular feedback

In your life, if someone comes and suggests feedback, first say thank you to them, whatever the content of their comments, because they have opened the first door for your correction. So show your humility and carefully listen to them, analyze them, and then reflect on them to correct yourself. Feedback and self-reflection are efficient techniques that help you grow professionally.

Uncertainty Handling

Nobody in the software industry guarantees 100% job security. Uncertainties will always be there, from interns to and CEOs (chief executive officers). Not only job security but uncertainties will also be there on projects, client requirements, or any new organizational updates (e.g., pay hikes). We can overcome such uncertainty if we have resilience and a strong mindset. You can reduce your anxiety if you are up to date with technologies with continuous learning which we will discuss in chapter 7.

Your Journey Starts Here!!

This book is your guide to mastering that evolution.

You'll discover practical techniques to:

- Overcome self-limiting beliefs

- Develop a **growth mindset**

- Set meaningful goals

- Build resilience

- Embrace change

- Strengthen emotional intelligence

- Craft your career vision

- Sharpen your problem-solving skills

- Track and measure your progress

- Build daily rituals

While this book is tailored for IT professionals, the lessons go far beyond tech.

They apply to **anyone determined to pursue excellence and live a meaningful, purpose-driven life.**

So let's begin.

The code to your success story is waiting to be written—**line by line.**

Chapter 1

Code Your Mindset: Diagnosing Current Limitations

In the programming world, when a tester or customer reports an issue, our first step is to thoroughly understand the problem. Generally, we dive into the root cause, analyse the situation, and then write code to resolve the issue. Similarly, in our careers, challenges often stem from limitations in our mindset—mental barriers that prevent us from progressing. One needs to take care to knock that off. By diagnosing these limitations, we can identify their root causes and apply effective strategies to overcome them, just as we debug and refine our code to make it more efficient and resilient.

This chapter will guide you through the process of *diagnosing, solving, and optimising* your mindset. Together, we'll identify the limitations that may be hindering your growth. Then we'll work on methods to overcome them and align your mindset with success.

Let's take a deep dive into identifying mental barriers and find a way to overcome them to achieve success.

1.1 Self-Assessment: Analysing Your Mental Framework

Whenever customers or QA report a problem in a software product, we (de)bug the code to find the problem before providing an elegant solution. Similarly, if we can apply the same concept to our mindset, it involves finding the problematic area in our mind. It requires self-assessment of your beliefs, habits, and behaviours and how they shape your career.

Assume you are a software developer, and whenever there is a problem to address, your approach to the problem determines the kind of mental framework, i.e., a set of beliefs and thoughts about yourself, your abilities, and your potential. When you have a fixed mindset, you will become overwhelmed by the complexity of the problem itself; instead of approaching a solution, you will spend time dwelling on *negative thoughts* about it. On the other hand, if you have a growth mindset, you will view the problem as an opportunity for growth and approach it positively. It aligns with **Carol Dweck's concept of fixed and growth mindsets**, as discussed earlier in the section *Decoding the Success Algorithm*.

Once you start analysing your mindset, you can identify potential issues or limiting beliefs that prevent you from taking risks, challenging yourself at work, opening up to others, learning new skills, and embracing new opportunities. During self-assessment, you need to be frank enough to observe the thought patterns that you get so that you can apply corrections to excel in your life.

One of the better ways to address this is to set aside a dedicated time for *self-reflection* wherein you can start questioning yourself like:

Number	Self- Assessment
1	What is my reaction to the problem? Did I work at my full potential?
2	Did I bias anything due to fear of rejection?
3	Do I have any takeaway Today? Can I reuse my learning on different occasions?
4	How could I have done it better?
5	Do I foresee any issues if I follow this approach?

Regularly practising self-assessment lets you observe your thought pattern, which can help you rewire your thoughts toward career success.

Now let's write our self-assessment details in the table:

Number	Self- Assessment
1	
2	
3	
4	
5	

1.2 Identifying Debugging Needs: Recognizing Limiting Beliefs And Challenging Our Thoughts

Bugs are unhealthy for any software product as they deviate from expected behaviour. The severity varies depending on the nature of the bug. Addressing defects early is essential for a better end-user experience. The concept of *limiting beliefs*—mental blocks that prevent us from reaching our full potential—has been widely discussed in the personal development world. Thought leaders like Tony Robbins have emphasised how these internal barriers can shape our reality and hold us back from meaningful growth and success (*Robbins, 2001*).

Limiting beliefs are like bugs in our minds, and eliminating them is a primary step to applying the success algorithm. Like doctors identify disease before they treat, it is necessary to locate limiting beliefs as a primary step.

Even in the software world, many people may hold limiting beliefs, and I had some myself during the early part of my career. Here are some of them:

- I don't think I have time for developing new skills

- It's harder to survive in the software architect role

- I guess I can't fix this bug

- A management role does not suit me.

- While reporting a bug, for god's sake, let this be a real bug

- I am afraid of losing my job if this feature does not work properly.

- My fix will not get through regression.

These statements reflect how our internal dialogue can quietly influence the way we think, decide, and respond in our professional journey. I've faced some of these thoughts myself early in my career. It is not the actual problem that holds us back, but the story that we repeatedly tell ourselves that holds us back. Limiting beliefs aren't facts—they're just outdated mental scripts.

To illustrate this, let me share an instance I faced during my early career days. I was working at a software company, and I developed a feature that went to QA for testing. It was those times when more bugs were considered severe by customers. I was scared that if this feature did not work in the QA environment, I would be laid off if the feature broke. Should I prepare for an interview to apply for the next job? It is *not the correct thinking*; why should someone lay off if something breaks? If so, fix it; this should have been my approach. *It is a sin to talk to our minds with such pessimistic remarks because this will make our subconscious believe it is true. In turn, our minds will provoke us to stay in that state longer, which is unhealthy for our career growth. So, it would be best to avoid them.* This aligns with the widely discussed idea in psychology that repetitive negative self-talk can influence subconscious beliefs and emotional patterns.

Now, the next question is how to recognize our limiting beliefs. The answer lies in paying close attention to our internal dialogue. Whenever you encounter a new task, like learning a new skill, presenting a topic to a large audience, or tackling anything that makes you hesitate—despite its potential to add positive value to your professional or personal life—take a moment to reflect.

Create a table with a column dedicated to your thoughts during these moments. Be **honest** with yourself as you write them down. Here's a simple template to guide you:

Situation/Task	Thoughts/Inner Dialogue
Learning a new programming language	"This is too hard for me; I'll never get it."
Presenting to a large audience	"What if I forget what to say? People will think I'm unprepared."
Applying for a leadership role	"I'm not experienced enough to manage a team."

By following this approach, you'll uncover recurring patterns in your thoughts—these are your **limiting beliefs**. Recognizing them is the first critical step toward addressing and overcoming them.

Now, in the table below, let's write our limiting beliefs in the below table.Is

Number	Limiting Beliefs
1	
2	
3	
4	
5	
6	
7	

Challenge Your Thoughts

Now challenge your thoughts by asking the following questions yourself:

- Is my fear or anxiety genuine?

- Does my belief on this occasion make sense?

- Do I have supporting evidence to prove my worry or anxiety?

- Can I take an alternative approach instead of worrying?

- Why should the company pay if I don't accept this challenge?

And many more...

The above techniques are inspired by **Cognitive Behavioural Therapy (CBT)**, a psychological framework developed by psychiatrist **Aaron T. Beck**. CBT focuses on :

a. identifying distorted or negative thought patterns and

b. **reframing** them to support healthier behaviours and emotional responses.

Now let's take an example:

Ananya, a talented senior software developer, was approached by her manager to handle a highly escalated issue in the company's product. Due to her **limiting beliefs**, her internal dialogue went something like this:

1. "Will I be able to handle this?"

    - *Underlying Limiting Belief:* "I'm not capable of solving critical issues," which triggered immediate nervousness and fear, undermining her confidence.

2. "Will I be able to find the root cause? Can I give daily updates? Will I make daily Progress?"

    - *Underlying Limiting Belief:* "I don't have the problem-solving skills to manage high-pressure situations effectively". Those doubts created intense pressure, making the task feel overwhelming before it even began.

3. "What if I don't resolve the issue? Will the company fire me?"

    - *Underlying Limiting Belief:* 'If I fail to do this task, it will lead to serious consequences.' Here she was worrying more about the consequences rather than putting her efforts into the issue. This line of thinking exacerbates her fear; her focus shifted to worst-case outcomes.

Ananya's internal dialogues reflected common **limiting beliefs** that many professionals may experience in modern times. She started writing down the thoughts and linking them to the deeper fears beneath; she could begin to see these patterns not as truths, but as **mental barriers** that she must overcome.

Using a CBT-inspired reframing technique, Ananya can rewrite her thoughts:

- From: "Will I be able to handle this?"

- To: "I have the skills and experience to take this one step at a time."

- From: "What if I can't make daily progress?"

- To: "Progress is a process. I'll put my sincere effort, stay consistent and communicate clearly."

- From: "What if I fail?"

- To: "This is a valuable opportunity to learn, grow, and show resilience."

Reflection Exercise for Ananya

Situation	Thought	Reframed Thoughts
Handling an escalated issue	"Will I be able to handle this?"	"I'll break the problem into manageable parts and focus."
Providing daily updates	"Can I progress every day?"	"Daily progress isn't about perfection; it's about effort."
Fear of consequences	"What if I fail and get fired?"	"This task is a challenge, not a judgment of my worth."

By consciously reframing her thoughts, Ananya could transform her anxiety into confidence and turn the escalated problem into an opportunity to showcase her abilities.

Such questions helped Ananya overcome her negative beliefs and proceed with analysing problems.

Now in the table below, challenge your thoughts and write in the below table:

Num	Thoughts or limiting beliefs	Reframed thoughts
1		
2		
3		
4		
5		

After writing, you can start taking the required actions.

Identifying *Fear of Failure* in our profession

In the software world, fear of failure is a common challenge. We often worry about missing feature deadlines, fixing critical bugs, or completing test cases—especially when we're unsure how to explain a delay. After delivering a feature, many of us anxiously wait, hoping it works as expected.

But is fear just about technical challenges? Not really. **Fear is often rooted in emotional responses.** It comes from our perception of a potential threat in the future, even if there's no clear evidence it will occur. These feelings may originate from:

- past experiences,

- lack of preparation,

- misunderstandings, or

- attachment to specific outcomes.

This aligns with **Martin Seligman's theory of learned helplessness (1975).** His research suggests that repeated exposure to failure or perceived lack of control can lead individuals to believe their actions no longer make a difference. Over time, this belief may cause them to avoid new challenges—even when they are capable of succeeding.

Fear can manifest in various ways:

- Procrastination

- Avoiding responsibilities or challenges

- Feeling anxious or mentally blocked before results arrive

Fear of failure may prevent us from:

- Taking on innovative or high-visibility projects

- Maintaining calm focus and creative thinking

- Building consistent progress

- Growing in self-confidence

Developing mindfulness around these fears helps us identify the internal dialogue and emotional triggers holding us back. In **Section 2.3.4**, we'll explore practical strategies to overcome these fears and build resilience.

Now, let's explore some exercises to help recognize and address fear of failure.

Num	Things which you afraid of failure	Identify WHY?	Can this be reframed similar to previous section?
1	Appearing for upcoming interview	Lack of preparation	Since my preparation is not very good, I should expect to fail. But I'm prepared, my preparation may not be perfect right now, so failure is possible—and that's okay. What matters more is that I'm **willing to learn, grow, and return stronger next time.**
2			

Num	Things which you afraid of failure	Identify WHY?	Can this be reframed similar to previous section?
3			
4			
5			

Identifying Career Stagnation in Our Profession

Have you ever felt like you've been in the same job for a long time, without learning anything new, struggling to acquire fresh skills or experiences? Perhaps your work no longer excites you, internal or external mobility feels out of reach, you feel undervalued, or promotions and significant salary hikes seem elusive. These could be signs that you're experiencing **career stagnation**. Who likes this? No one!!

When we reflect on the causes of career stagnation, **the comfort zone** often emerges as a primary factor. Success usually requires us to **step beyond what feels safe or familiar**. During crisis times, such as a layoff, this can be extremely costly.

Here are a few common causes of career stagnation that professionals often face:

- **Lack of a clear career vision** - simply going with the flow

- **Fear of change** - hesitation in embracing new challenges

- **Fear of failure**- afraid of mistakes, or avoiding professional risks

- Ignoring **continuous skill development** over time

If you identify with any of these challenges, don't worry. This book offers solutions and guidance on goal setting, skill development, embracing feedback, finding mentors, and building robust professional networks.

Now, let's do some exercises to reflect on your career journey and identify areas where you may be experiencing stagnation.

Num	Do you feel you fall under career stagnation?	Identify WHY?	Can this be reframed similar to previous section?
1	I am struggling to move across projects.	My current skills are not sufficient which new project need.	I will proactively upskill myself to meet the evolving demands of future projects.
2			
3			
4			
5			

Note: Imposter syndrome also falls under problematic areas but we will discuss this in future chapters

1.3 Visualizing Your Code Path: Creating a Mind Map of Success

In most cases, whenever we identify the root cause of a bug in our code or a bottleneck in our project, the next step is to resolve it using the most effective and efficient approach. Similarly, when we recognize limiting beliefs or mental blocks that hinder our professional growth, the solution lies in visualizing a clear path to overcome them.

One powerful method for mapping this journey is through a **mind map**—a widely adopted technique popularised by Tony Buzan in *The Mind Map Book*. A *mind map* allows you to break down a larger end goal into smaller, actionable steps. It helps to visualise mentally each stage of progress. Just like a roadmap for our brain, a mind map provides both direction and clarity.

Let's say your goal is: **"Becoming a Software Development Manager."** Instead of treating it as one overwhelming objective, you can branch it into smaller, manageable tasks as mentioned below mindmap:

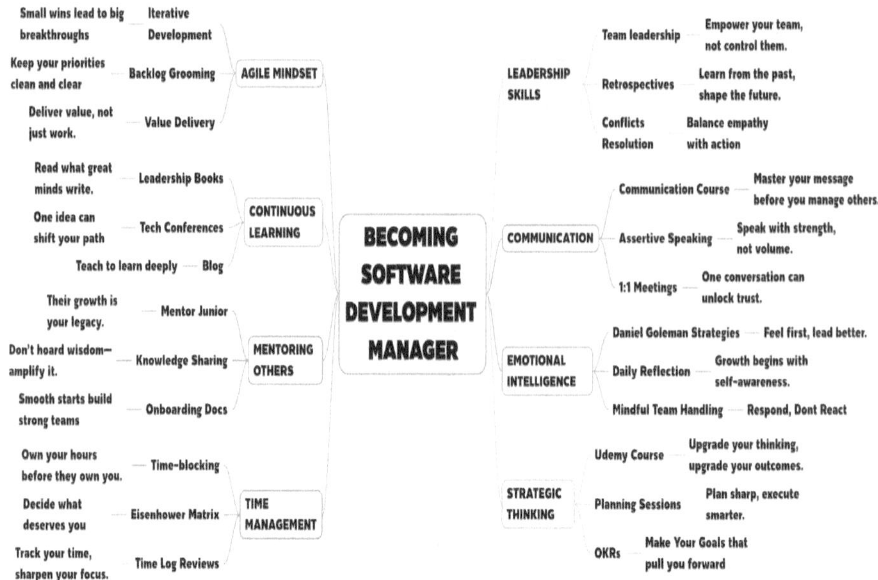

Figure 1.1: Mind map inspired by Tony Buzan's method. Visual hierarchy is conveyed via font size, casing, and layout because of black-and-white print constraints and current tool (Boardmix) familiarity.

Brief note on mindmap information references:

Leadership Skills

- *Emphasizing servant leadership and emotional intelligence aligns with Daniel Goleman's work on leadership and self-awareness (Goleman, 1995).*

Communication

- *Effective communication and assertiveness are essential skills that can be developed through focused learning, as outlined in leadership communication resources.*

Emotional Intelligence

- *Daily reflection and mindful responses are practices rooted in the principles of emotional intelligence popularized by Daniel Goleman (Goleman, 1995).*

Strategic Thinking

- *Using OKRs (Objectives and Key Results) for goal setting is a widely adopted framework pioneered by John Doerr (Doerr, 2018).*

Agile Mindset

- Inspired by the *Manifesto for Agile Software Development* (2001), Agile methodology emphasises iterative progress and continuous adaptation, allowing teams to quickly respond to change and focus on delivering tangible value at every step.

Continuous Learning

- *Continuous improvement through reading, conferences, and teaching aligns with lifelong learning concepts embraced by many leadership thought leaders.*

Mentoring Others

- *Knowledge sharing and mentoring build legacy and team strength, reflecting best practices in leadership development.*

Time Management

- *Techniques such as time-blocking and the Eisenhower Matrix are practical tools for prioritisation and focus (Covey, 1989).*

Let's now take each of these branches and turn them into real, actionable goals using the S.M.A.R.T. approach. Every letter stands for something powerful: **Specific, Measurable, Achievable, Relevant,** and **Time-bound**. This is a simple - yet impactful concept introduced by George T. Doran in 1981 in *Management Review, 70(11), 35–36,* and it has since become a trusted tool for anyone serious about setting and achieving meaningful goals. You'll see us use this framework often throughout the book—it's a game-changer.

For example:

- **Decision-Making**: Enrol in a Udemy or Coursera course on decision-making within the next two weeks and complete it over the next three months.

- **Empathy**: Practice active empathy during daily stand-up meetings and retrospectives. Track your impact over the next six months through peer feedback.

- **Communication**: Join a communication enhancement program by the next quarter and apply key learnings in team sync-ups.

- **Mentorship**: Start mentoring a junior team member on a weekly basis for at least 30 minutes. Track their progress and your learning through a shared log.

Each of these goals is not just theoretical—they are action-driven, time-bound, and personalised to your development.

Once these SMART goals are created, place them under their respective branches in in the mind map which you created for your goal. This structure will help you **track progress** and maintain clarity on where you're headed. Just as we use Git commits to track every code change, your mind map will reflect every milestone on your growth journey.

A mind map is not just a technique—it's your **career blueprint**. It empowers you to stay focused, motivated, and organised. It gives your vision a shape, your actions a purpose, and your future a direction.

Note: The skillsets outlined in the mind map are just a sample of what is needed to become a project manager. Many more skills are required for success in this and other career paths, which will be explored in next version of **"The Success Algorithm"** in upcoming book.

Summary

In this chapter, the metaphor of programming is used to understand and improve your mindset. Just as bugs in code need to be identified and fixed, this chapter helps you identify and overcome mental barriers that hinder your career growth. It is divided into three key areas:

1.1 Self-Assessment: Analysing Your Mental Framework

- Treat your mindset like software that requires debugging.

- Reflect on your beliefs, habits, and behaviours to identify what might hold you back.

- Adopt a positive, growth-oriented approach to challenges instead of being overwhelmed by negativity.

- Regular self-assessment through honest questions (e.g., "How could I have handled this better?") helps you correct thought patterns and build a better mindset.

1.2 Recognizing Limiting Beliefs

- Limiting beliefs are like mental "bugs" that stop you from achieving your potential.

- These negative thoughts, such as fear of failure or self-doubt, should be identified early and actively challenged.

- Replace harmful internal dialogue with constructive questions, such as, "Why not trust me if others do?" or "Let me turn this challenge into an opportunity for growth?"

- An example is shared about a software developer overcoming anxiety by addressing her negative thoughts with logical and empowering questions.

1.3 Creating a Mind Map of Success

- Once limiting beliefs are identified, visualize your success path, like creating a project blueprint.

- Break down larger career goals into smaller, actionable steps using the SMART framework (Specific, Measurable, Achievable, Relevant, and Time-bound).

- Regularly track your progress so as to get motivated and master the skills needed for success.

This chapter equips readers with practical tools to "debug" their mindset and build a foundation for personal and professional growth in the software industry.

Chapter 2

Refactoring Your Thinking: Upgrading to a Growth Mindset

"thamsoma jyothirgamaya" is a Sanskrit quote that translates to
"lead me from darkness towards light."

– Brhadaranyaka Upanishad 1.3.28

Refactoring is a term used in software development to refer to optimising code without altering its original behaviour. This task is required if we need to make the code - cleaner, more efficient, and easier to understand.

Similarly, refactoring is required to adapt positive attitudes and thinking patterns. It is essential to meet new challenges in the fast-paced IT industry. Technology is constantly evolving, but our mindset often remains fixed. To keep up with modern technology, we must upgrade the tools, frameworks, programming languages, and development methodologies we used decades ago. Staying current in our careers requires transforming from a fixed(static) mindset to a growth mindset.

In Chapter 1, we learnt the importance of Carol's growth mindset, especially in the IT field. Here, we can see how to apply it. Innovations often occur once we adopt a growth mindset. It's all about embracing constant change and viewing it as an opportunity to grow, rather than a burden.

We can apply the basic concept of a growth mindset, which involves forming a strong belief that you can learn anything through continuous and persistent effort. In that case, coping with ongoing modern trends should be easy. Additionally, affirmations(positive statements) can help you grow in the right direction. We also need to overcome even traces of a fixed mindset. Most of the professionals I have encountered so far are moving towards a growth mindset, so never hesitate to adopt it.

Like our personal life, shaping your professional life is entirely in your hands. The more effort you put towards growth, the better your life will be. It is often the case that when working on ongoing projects with hectic schedules, it is challenging for all of us to find time to upgrade to new technologies. If you procrastinate on new learning, it will cost you a lot. People with a fixed mindset *(as defined by Carol Dweck)* tend to postpone new learning. If you procrastinate for more than a week on any new learning, you might never spend your effort on that again. In Sanskrit, there is a popular proverb which I heard since childhood: "*Shubhastya sheegram*", which translates to "One should not postpone good actions". So, kindly apply this to your learning as well.

Suppose you are a working software professional who uses time management techniques, which most people with a growth mindset do. In that case, you can still make time to upgrade yourself.

Aakash, a software professional at a Tech Giant, used to spend almost an hour commuting to work. He used a train to reach his office. Many of us sleep, especially during the commute, but Akash has a different approach.

During his commutes, he used that one hour to listen to Amazon Web Services(AWS) training through Udemy courses. By the end of six months, he had cracked one of the AWS certification exams. Isn't he a great example for all of us?

The above scenario is just one example. This chapter has three main sections. Let's discuss adopting a flexible mindset (Section 2.1) and eliminating negative thoughts (Section 2.2). and continuous improvement(2.3) in this chapter.

2.1 From Fixed to Agile: Embracing Flexibility in Thinking

When I say **'Agile'** in this paragraph, I don't just mean the software development model; it's a way of thinking—a mindset that bends, adapts, and flows. Agile means being open to change, learning as you go, and adjusting when things don't go as planned. It's the mindset we need not to embrace—not just to survive—but to **thrive** in the ever-changing tech world.

Earlier in this book, I discussed Carol's **growth mindset**. Now let's take that further. Because if you're stuck in a fixed mindset—believing that your skills are limited, that you either "have it or you don't"—you're going to struggle. You might resist learning new things, ignore feedback, and shy away from challenges. And honestly, that's a mindset that holds you back both professionally and personally.

But here's the truth: change is uncomfortable. It feels like stepping into the unknown. You might remember those moments—during your school days or first job—when learning something new felt like climbing a mountain. But looking back, wasn't that discomfort worth it?

It's like medicine—bitter at first, but healing in the end.

If you want to grow, lead, and make a mark in this field, you have to build the habit of embracing change. Below are a few simple but powerful habits that helped me and others I've worked with.

◈ *1. See Challenges as Growth Chances*

Let's face it—challenges are scary. When you get a tough task, your first thought might be, "Why me?" But pause. Consider this as an opportunity for your learning and growth. Ask mentors, dig deep, and give your full effort. And once you crack it—no matter how small—it gives you a real sense of progress.

📝 *Tip from my journey: always jot down how you solved something. That's how experience builds. That's how you become someone others look up to.*

◈ *2. Don't Fear Failure—Expect It*

Failure is part of the process. I've failed so many times, I've lost count. But each failure pointed me to a better solution. So if something doesn't work? Rethink it. Tweak your approach. Try again. That's how real learning happens.

◈ *3. Stay Open-Minded*

When you're stuck, don't limit yourself. Don't say, "This is the only way I know." Be curious. Think sideways. Try small experiments. The more open you are, the more creative your ideas will be.

"A river of good ideas flows to those who keep their minds open." – Something I've learned the hard way.

◈ *4. Take Risks and Spark Creativity*

No invention happens without risk. Whether it's building a new tool, suggesting a new feature, or learning a new language, there's always a risk. You might fail. But if you don't try, you don't grow.

A saying in Sanskrit that I've heard since I was a child:

"Dhairyam Sarvatra Sadhanam" – *With courage, everything is possible.* *"Don't fear thinking differently. Don't fear trying."*

◈ *5. Be Ahead of Change—Not Behind It*

I once read *Who Moved My Cheese?* by Dr. Spencer Johnson. It talks about preparing for change instead of being caught off guard.

Let me provide a real-world example.

Sherlyn, a Staff Software Engineer at a top company, was working on regular backend stuff. But she sensed that **Cloud Computing** was going to boom. She didn't wait. She began learning cloud tools on her own, even without a project in hand. And guess what? Months later, when her team got a new cloud project, she was the only one ready—and she was asked to lead it.

That's how preparation meets opportunity.

"Without karma, nothing moves—and every noble effort bears fruit in time."

◈ *6. Keep Learning. Always.*

I met a trainer once—must have been over 80 years old—but he had more energy than most of us. When I asked how he stays so sharp, he smiled and said:

"I keep learning every single day."

He also told me:

"We must keep learning until our last breath."
That stuck with me. Since then, my mantra has been simple:
"Learning. Learning. And more learning."

◈ *7. Build Your Circle of Creative Thinkers*

Your environment matters. If thinkers, innovators, and learners surround you, you'll grow faster. If not, think about what works for you. Be part of a group that pushes you, supports you, and expects greatness from you. You'll start to think better just by being around them.

◈ *8. Celebrate Small Wins*

Not every victory has to be big. Solving a bug, learning a new command, completing a course—these are all wins. I used to celebrate those small wins when I was just starting. They gave me the energy to keep going.

"Celebrate your small success. It doesn't cost you anything—but it fuels everything."

◈ *9. Love What You Do*

If you're in tech, ask yourself—do I love what I do? If not, develop that love. No passion? No progress. Passion makes you try, fail, and try again. It's what separates someone who survives from someone who **leads**.

"If you're waiting for a perfect day to start loving your work, stop. The perfect day is today."

2.2 Uninstalling Negative Code: Removing Limiting Narratives

Bugs are common in software, but it is essential to eliminate them with the correct code. Similarly, limiting thoughts and beliefs threaten our career success.

So, they need to expel the limiting beliefs from their minds. The next question is how to get rid of them. In Chapter 1, we saw examples of such thoughts. Being a software developer, at least we have some idea of how to eliminate bugs in the area where we work. Similarly, we also need to remove bugs that hinder our progress from our thoughts.

Here are a few strategies: a. Identify limiting beliefs; b. Challenge the beliefs; and c. Replace them with empowering beliefs.

Kindly refer to Chapter 2 for details about the above cognitive beliefs.

2.3 Writing New Scripts: Strategies for Continuous Improvement

In software development, we use scripts to automate tasks and make them more accessible. But here, scripts refer to mental patterns. We need to adopt mental scripts that fuel continuous improvement and growth.

Figure 3.2: Continuous improvement

Here are a few strategies:

Adoptive the Mentality of Learning

Continuous learning is a must for constant improvement. So, tune your mind to learn continuously. A Sanskrit proverb I learned during my high school days says, **"Vidwan Sarvatra Poojyathe"**—*A learned person is respected everywhere.* If you want to thrive in software, keep learning according to trends or project needs. This makes you adaptable and relevant. We will learn more about this in Chapter 7 of this book.

Set Learning Goals

If you want to enhance or learn new skills, you need to have learning goals, both short-term and long-term. You can split larger goals into shorter goals. Use the George T. Doran's **S.M.A.R.T.** framework to do so. Take action on them. Also, it creates a sense of urgency to achieve them. Note: We will discuss this in the upcoming chapter.

Embrace feedback

Feedback is essential for everyone in the software field to grow. It helps assess strengths, areas for improvement, and required corrective actions. Feedback is necessary for everyone, regardless of age or position.

Practice Mindfulness

Mindfulness is the awareness of one's thoughts and emotions. It enables an individual to take control of the mind and consciously guide actions in the right direction.

Rooted in ancient practices, mindfulness is now supported by scientific research that highlights its positive effects on mental well-being. For example, Jon Kabat-Zinn's pioneering work was foundational in bringing mindfulness into clinical psychology.

Software professionals need to practice mindfulness because it helps to:

- Improve concentration and focus

- Reduce stress and anxiety

- Enhance emotional regulation

- Support better mental health

- Boost productivity

- Foster creativity and communication

- Increase self-awareness and resilience to challenges

and so on.

Some of the tips for software professionals:

a. **Daily Mindfulness Practice**: Before or during work, start with a few minutes of meditation or mindfulness breathing exercises to clear the mind and set intentions for the day.

b. **Mindful Coding**: Focus on one task at a time, paying full attention to the code you're writing and the problem you're solving, whether it's a script, an email, or anything else.

c. **Take Breaks**: Take mindful breaks by stepping away from your screen and focusing on your well-being. This simple practice refreshes your mind and helps prevent burnout. One effective way to organise these breaks is the *Pomodoro Technique*—a time management method created by *Francesco Cirillo* that encourages working in focused bursts followed by short, refreshing pauses (Cirillo, 2018).

d. **Emotional Check-ins**: Regularly assess your emotional state and practice techniques like deep breathing or journaling.

For all breathing-related and meditation techniques, I recommend that you seek advice from a well-known authority or certified practitioner before starting to practice.

Celebrate Progress

It is vital to celebrate progress to motivate ourselves to move further in our accomplishments. If you are leading a team, appreciate individual team members after every accomplishment. It will boost their confidence and energize them to reach the end goal correctly. You can also celebrate achieving personal goals. When you achieve smaller goals, reward yourself by going out with family or friends or spending quality time with them. Ask them if they are okay with listening to you which will help you move forward to towards the end goal.

Summary

The chapter draws inspiration from the Sanskrit quote *"Thamasoma Jyothirgamaya"* (from darkness to light), comparing upgrading one's mindset to refactoring in software development. Just as code is optimized without altering functionality, we must refine our thinking to adapt to the dynamic IT industry.

Thriving in a rapidly evolving field requires a *growth mindset*—the understanding that intelligence and abilities can be cultivated through continuous learning and dedicated effort. This mindset helps professionals embrace change, tackle challenges, and overcome procrastination. The chapter emphasizes that resisting new learning can lead to stagnation, while continuous improvement fuels long-term success.

Key Sections:

- **From Fixed to Agile: Embracing Flexibility in Thinking**

  Adapting an agile mindset involves seeing challenges as opportunities, accepting failures, staying open-minded, and fostering creativity. The section encourages professionals to:

  - Anticipate and prepare for change.

  - Celebrate small wins and maintain passion for their work.

  - Surround themselves with creative thinkers and continue lifelong learning.

- **Uninstalling Negative Code: Removing Limiting Narratives**

  Negative thoughts, akin to software bugs, can hinder growth. These must be identified, challenged, and replaced with empowering beliefs. Strategies to overcome these barriers were introduced in Chapter 2 and revisited here.

- **Writing New Scripts: Strategies for Continuous Improvement**

This section offers actionable steps for ongoing growth:

  - Set learning goals using the S.M.A.R.T. framework.

  - Seek feedback for self-assessment and improvement.

  - Practice mindfulness to maintain focus and direction.

  - Celebrate progress to sustain motivation and team morale.

The chapter concludes with real-life examples, such as a software professional utilizing commuting time to earn certifications and others embracing change to excel in their careers. The overall message is *by cultivating a growth mindset, embracing challenges, and continuously upgrading skills, professionals can ensure career success.*

Chapter 3

Agile Goal Setting: Navigating Your Software Career

"Goals are the compass that guide us on our journey, while agility is the wind that propels and steers us toward success. Without a clear direction, we drift; without agility, we cannot adapt to changing winds."

Professionals must set and achieve clear goals to thrive in the fast-evolving software industry. Without defined goals, individuals risk stagnating in their careers or feeling lost in their professional journeys. Goal setting serves as a roadmap, guiding professionals to acquire new skills, advance in their careers, and maintain long-term motivation. It is essential to be proactive in shaping your career path to ensure growth and fulfilment.

Much like the Agile methodology, this chapter delves into the process of setting **SMART** goals—Specific, Measurable, Achievable, Relevant, and Time-bound. We will explore how to break down long-term aspirations into smaller, manageable milestones, track progress, and make adjustments to short-term goals to stay on course and continuously advance in your career. Let's dive deeper into these principles and strategies.

3.1 Setting SMART Goals for Software Professionals: George T. Doran's Framework for Software Professionals

Goal setting is not just about you are wishing about something you want or something you obtain; it's about defining specific, tangible outcomes that steer your actions and decisions. Goals like "become a DevOps specialist" or "improve strategic thinking" serve as starting points, but to truly make progress, you need a more structured approach to turn these aspirations into actionable and impactful objectives. A well-defined goal provides clarity, offering a clear direction and a concrete path to reach your desired destination. Below are key guidelines to help you set goals that drive meaningful progress:

Specific: As the name indicates, your goal needs to be specific. For example, instead of setting vague goals like "I want to gain skill sets to apply for a Software Architect position," specify what you want to achieve, such as " I want to master software architecture for cloud systems and obtain the TOGAF 9 certification or an equivalent within the next six months."

Measurable: To ensure your goals are actionable, you need clear criteria to track progress and success. For example, " I will successfully design and document the architecture for the containerization project and receive feedback from peers and stakeholders within the next nine months."

Achievable: We must set realistic goals relevant to our skills and achievable timelines. For example, "Participate in or lead at least three architecture review meetings on cloud system with senior architects or stakeholders within the next six months."

Relevant: Your goals and career aspirations should align with each other. If your long-term goal is to become a Software Architect specializing in Cloud-Native Systems, aim to gain hands-on experience by implementing cloud-based solutions using platforms like AWS, Azure, GCP, or others in at least two projects over the next 12 months. Here, improving non relevant skills may not directly contribute to your career progression.

Time-bound: Every goal should have its timeline. A clear deadline adds urgency and keeps you accountable. Instead of saying, "I want to become a senior architect," say, "I will develop and present a strategic architecture proposal for an upcoming cloud native project to the engineering and management within the next year."

So, a SMART framework will convert your problem statement into specific, measurable, actionable and time-bound goals. Tailoring a target with a timeline often creates urgency and triggers consistent action.

Now, let's write down our goals using the above framework for Python learning in 6 months.

Number	Task	Target Days or Date for completion	Actual Date or Days for completion
1	Research materials like Udemy, various books	One day	
2	Learning Concepts through Online Resources	30	
3	Mini Projects	89	
4	Certification	60	

Note:

a. You can break down each task further at your convenience. For example, you can mention every concept one day and track it.

b. In the above table, python learning is just an example. You can add skill that you are passionate about and follow the template.

c. You can reuse the above table when you start learning new skill of your interest.

These are just examples—you can apply the same principles in your own context, whether in technical or non-technical areas, regardless of your age, experience, or position.

3.2 Sprint Planning: Breaking Down Long-Term Goals into Manageable Tasks

Sprint Planning is part of the Agile Development process. In sprint planning, larger tasks, usually called "epics," are subdivided into smaller tasks called "stories. " These stories are manageable tasks that must be completed within a fixed time, usually three or four weeks, depending on convenience.

Here is sprint-based approach to career development is illustrated through a case study focused on goal setting in a shopping cart application project, where the primary objective is implementing containerization.

Case Study: Goal setting for a technical interview, a small demo on breaking long-term goals into short-term goals:

The following is an illustrative example of how we can set goals for technical interview preparation for a software developer. If a developer is not at all prepared for the interview, he needs at least 3 – 6 months of preparation work. Let's assume, in the worst case, we need 6 months of interview preparation, which is our main long-term goal (your niche).

Everyone has their own career aspirations, and they can set their long-term goals accordingly. For example, they may desire to get new roles, change projects to stay up to date with market trends, change jobs for various reasons, etc. You can apply this technique to your own case. The main intention is to show how you can break your long-term goals into actionable steps.

Mathew, a software development engineer, aspired to get a new job. He appeared for an interview without preparation but failed miserably. Then, he came up with the following plan.

Objective: *Preparing for the interview of his dream company*

He broke objectives into high-level epics. We need to assign a time duration for each epic and make sure everything is covered within a net of six months.

Note: It depends on each individual. If you feel that you need to spend little more time on your domain and projects, feel free to extend your final goal before you start. Also here I am taking an example of Go programming language along with other relevant things required to face interview. Feel free to take examples of your own interest or aspirations.

To build concurrent and scalable applications, many engineers today turn to Go—an open-source language created at Google in 2009 [Google, 2009]. Go is known for its minimalism, efficient memory management, and built-in support for concurrency through goroutines

Epic(s)	Name of the epics
1	Developing proficiency in Go programming language
2	Build a deep understanding of Data Structures and Algorithms
3	Hands-on coding and problem solving using algorithms
4	Mastering system design concepts
5	Gathering knowledge about your previous accomplishments
6	Refreshing domain knowledge
7	Preparation for behavior interviews.
8	Mock Interviews and feedback

You are your own scrum master. While you can allocate time based on personal convenience, ensuring sufficient time is dedicated to Epics 3 and 4 is essential, as these areas typically require more effort, especially if you are relatively new to them. Now each epics can be broken individual user stories. I am taking the example of Epic 1.

User Stories	Name of the user stories
1	Identifying proper resources for Go programming
2	Learn basics of Go with hands-on experience
3	Develop expertise in Go functions and various error handling techniques
4	Mastering Go core features – Goroutines, Structs and Interfaces
5	Manging projects with Go modules and Packages
6	Building real world projects and testing the same with Go

You can expand other epics in your style. If you are using Atlassian's JIRA, we can have corresponding tickets for each of the above items.

Further, you can categorise into individual sub-tasks. For example: For the user story *(2) Learn basics of Go with hands-on experience* in the Epic 1: *Developing proficiency in Go programming language*, we can have below sub-tasks:

Sub tasks	Name of the sub tasks
1	Setting up environment for development for running Go programming
2	Write and run your first "Hello Go!!" program
3	Get familiarise with data types and variables – practice examples
4	Explore Control Flow mechanism in Go – with practice

You can expand other user stories in your style. If you use Atlassian's JIRA, we can have corresponding tickets for each item above.

Sample Time Allocation Aligned with Our Long-Term Goal

- Assume you have six months (~24 weeks) to complete these tasks.

- Each sprint lasts two weeks, giving you a total of 12 sprints.

- For simplicity, we can divide the work into two phases:

- **Phase One:** Sprints 1 to 6—focusing on Epics 1, 2, and 3.

- **Phase Two:** Sprints 7 to 12—focusing on Epics 4, 5, 6, 7, and 8.

Note: Fewer epics are planned in Phase One because Epic 3 is expected to require more time and is a core part of your interview preparation as a software developer. Similarly, Epic 4 in Phase Two may also need additional focus. Feel free to adjust the schedule according to your pace and learning needs.

Consider Epic 1: "Developing Proficiency in Go Programming Language."

By breaking it down into six user stories, we can plan this epic across Sprint 1 and Sprint 2.

- In **Sprint 1**, we aim to complete the first four user stories focusing on foundational Go concepts.

- **Sprint 2** addresses the remaining two stories, which dive into advanced features or practical applications.

Taking **User Story 2** as an example, we can further break it down into sub-tasks or sub-stories planned over a two-day window.

This same approach can be applied to the rest of the user stories—creating a consistent, manageable, and iterative path to mastery.

Note: It's just an example, it's up to you how you can plan your 6 months for your interview using above framework.

You can use this method to break larger tasks into smaller ones and track them using the Kanban board. The tasks include learning any programming languages, operating systems, scripts, DevOps tools, soft skills like strategic thinking, negotiation, leadership, cost estimation, accounting, etc and management skills and many more depending on your or your organisation requirement. It will be an organised and more effective process while accompanying your task.

You can use the below template to accomplish your task:

Primary Intent or Epic:

____

Now, split the primary intent into different epics:

1	
2	
3	
4	
5	

Now split epics into different user stories:

1	
2	
3	
4	
5	
6	
7	
8	
9	
10	

Now, start working on each user story. If you have access to Jira, you can create separate tickets to organize work and track progress effectively. Also, you can split further into different sub-stories

1	
2	
3	
4	
5	

Sprint Task prioritization

During the sprint plan, setting priorities for the tasks is essential. Priority decides the execution order of tasks. Scrum masters ensure they push to execute very high-priority tasks first. Setting priorities depends on business needs. In the above example, stories of epic "*Developing proficiency in Go programming language*" will get the highest priority, as they became the starting point for interview preparation in that example. Usually, the scrum master or product owner(In the above example yourself) will prioritize epics and stories.

As an exercise, if you create tasks as mentioned in the previous section, you can prioritize them based on your needs.

Set Task Durations

The usual sprint duration is three or four weeks. As mentioned earlier, it all depends on the individual project or organization. You can use this organization's learning system.

Example: In the above example, we have set sprint duration as two weeks, as only one person is involved in the entire process. If you create your own stories, you can customize the duration for each task and start working on them.

Tracking Sprint Progress

It is most important to track sprint progress. In the sprint meeting, we need to mention what we did yesterday and what we will do Today. We also need to make sure whether we are blocked on a task we are doing and what the action item is to overcome that.

The same technique can be applied to our learnings as well. Audit your sprint tasks daily and ensure you are on the right track. If not, identify the blockage and, if possible, solve it. Otherwise, find alternatives.

Complete your interview preparation or any other thing that you wrote as planned. If any blockages, like an internet connectivity issue, occur during learning, go for a physical handbook. The main intention is to keep the workflow intact.

To monitor your progress effectively, you can use online tools like JIRA

3.3 Retrospectives: Learning from Progress and Adjusting Goals

Usually, some companies that follow Agile methodologies conduct retrospective meetings at the end of every sprint. It is a self-reflection sprint; the scrum master consults with members to discuss on accomplishments and areas of improvement. The idea is not to blame anyone but to take corrective action to achieve the end goal. They take the team's suggestions and apply corrective actions. We can use the same principles in the personal life journey as well.

You can cultivate a similar Agile technique to your learning goal. Review your journey at the end of the designated sprint, document how it is progressing, and consider making corrections if it needs to be on the right track to the final goal.

Celebrate yourself on Successful Accomplishments:

In your retrospective, make time to appreciate yourself for completing tasks on time. Journal what went well and ask yourself:

	Questionnaire	Yes or No	If yes, document your idea for future purpose
1	Can I apply this approach to other occasions, too?		
2	Did I complete all my goals effectively?		
3	How confident am I in the topics I have learnt?		

Recognizing accomplishments will Recognize positive notes and motivate us to proceed more enthusiastically.

Analysis of incomplete tasks:

In our retrospective, we visualize or think about what we visualize planned. Check if you understand your technology sufficiently on the topics planned. Try to take some tests to check your knowledge. In case you feel you are lagging, ask yourself similar to below questions:

	Self-questionnaire	Yes/No	If Yes, corrective action
1	Am I spending too much time on a single task?		
2	Am I procrastinating or not following learning rituals?		
3	Am I getting sufficient time for learning?		
4	Am I underloaded or overloaded?		
5	Does health issue hamper my learning?		
6	Are there any other external reasons?		

When you find the answers to these questions, you will understand why you could not complete the task in the sprint and will be guided in taking appropriate action.

The moment when you realise the answers to above questions, you will find the reason for not completing the task in the current sprint and will be guided to take appropriate action.

Anomalies Corrections in Sprint Tasks

Like in any other field, we can see anomalies in sprint task completion as well. As an instance, specific tasks may miss the sprint timeline or certain tasks may need to be completed within the time limit.

So, the scrum master must ensure that sprint tasks are adjusted accordingly. They must check a task's accuracy and, based on that, need to apply corrections to subsequent tasks.

You can apply the same techniques to executing learning tasks. There could be chances that you might skip your learning timeline due to other priority tasks that what you planned. Feel free to adjust your tasks accordingly.

Summary

This chapter concentrates on the importance of goal setting and how it plays a vital role in navigating and shaping a successful career. It illustrates how we can avoid career stagnation and maintain long-term motivation to achieve our goals. Inspired by principles of AGILE methodologies, this chapter offers a systematic approach to defining, breaking down, and attaining professional goals or aspirations.

- 3.1 Setting SMART Goals: The SMART framework systematically converts an abstract aspiration into real-time achievable action items. It demonstrates, with examples like obtaining certifications and developing new skills, how clear and precise goals can create a roadmap for career advancement.

- 3.2 Sprint Planning: Inspired by Agile sprint cycles, this section shows how to break long-term goals into smaller, manageable tasks. Using a shopping cart containerization project case study, it illustrates dividing epics into user stories and subtasks, prioritizing them based on dependencies, and tracking progress with tools like Kanban boards. This approach ensures that we can make steady progress and adaptability.

- 3.3 Retrospectives: The chapter demonstrates how regular reflection at the end of sprints helps assess progress, identify obstacles and celebrate achievements. Self-analysis questions guide professionals in diagnosing delays and improving workflows. Adjusting strategies based on retrospectives ensures continuous improvement.

By adopting these Agile-inspired techniques, professionals can navigate their careers methodically, achieving goals effectively while staying motivated and adaptable to industry demands.

Chapter 4

Debugging Challenges: Cultivating Resilience

"The sharpest sword is forged in the hottest furnace."

– Anonymous Proverb

In software development, debugging is essential for analysing issues to identify their root cause and provide an appropriate solution. Similarly, challenges are common across all areas of the software industry. Every team in an organisation encounters obstacles in software development, QA, IT operations, HR, finance, or any other group. Here, the key is to understand the actual root cause of the problem and develop resilience to counteract the same. Despite having challenges, resilience enables professionals to maintain focus and drive toward success.

Figure 4.1: Cultivating Resilience

Cultivating resilience means returning from obstacles and building a solid mind to excel in an adverse environment and move towards a goal. In 4.1, we focus on common barriers in a software career and methods to overcome them. 4.2 mentions building strong mental toughness and resilience, and 4.3 discusses bouncing back from failures and learning from setbacks.

4.1 Common Obstacles in Software Careers and How to Overcome Them

Software life is not as smooth as it appears from the outside. Everyone in this field, from interns to CEOs (chief executive officers), often faces one or more obstacles in daily life and challenges in their roles. In this section, we will discuss the common challenges many professional faces and strategies for overcoming them.

Challenge-1: Rapid change in technology

As mentioned earlier several times, the software industry is dynamic. Technology changes rapidly, including programming languages, operating system flavours, frameworks, software tools, evolving ideas, processes and methodologies, innovations, optimizations leveraging resources, etc. Adopting such change sometimes becomes overwhelming. Some professionals often struggle to cope with this change, and it is essential to know how to react to it to thrive in software life.

Counteractions:

a. **Continuous learning**: In software life, learning is a never-ending process. You need to develop a constant learning attitude about emerging technologies. These can be a new programming language, framework, or technology. Individuals can achieve this through online learning by enrolling in courses on learning platforms like Udemy, Coursera, etc. or even reading books, blogs, or some websites. Some people prefer physical books as well. Set a goal mentioned in the previous chapter and work towards it.

b. **Seeking community support**: Another way to learn is to join online forums like GitHub, Reddit, Stack Overflow, etc., and learn about your topic of interest. In some organizations, there will be an internal community where open discussions will be held on various issues. You can subscribe to them to learn more.

Platforms like Coursera, Udemy, GitHub, and Stack Overflow are widely used for continuous learning and community support.

Challenge-2: Professional fatigue

Professional fatigue is a common problem in today's fast paced work environment. Professionals often work longer hours to meet tight deadlines, eventually stressing themselves out. Some people will not take breaks, making things much harder.

Counteractions:

a. **Work-life Balance:** Every professional needs a personal life regardless of role, position, or experience level. Our personal lives provide the foundation for our professional drive. On other hand, our work supports our individual lives and families. So, both are interdependent, and neglecting either of them will trouble us one or other way. Balancing professional responsibilities and individual well-being is vital for long-term success and fulfilment. Here are the strategies we can use for balancing between professional life and personal life:

   - **Set Boundaries:** Establish clear boundaries between work and personal life. Avoid distractions during your designated work hours. For more details, refer to the "Set Hour" section of "Create a Structured Daily Schedule:" in chapter 13.

   - **Schedule Personal Time:** Plan a dedicated time for personal activities, hobbies, and relaxation. It may be a workout, spiritual, or spending time with loved ones or friends. Engaging in enjoyable activities helps reduce stress and improves your overall well-being. Too much is too bad, so plan how much time you need to spend on these.

b. **Time-blocking technique:**

   - **Block Time for Specific Tasks:** A few people said, "We don't have time to read, enhance skills, work out, etc." It is all because they are not allocating time for these tasks. They may think these things are not critical, but they must allocate time. Make sure to allocate dedicated time blocks for specific tasks or activities.

     For example, set aside time in the morning for focused work and time in the afternoon for meetings or collaborative projects.

- **Multitasking**: Concentrate on one task at a time during each time block. Multitasks can reduce productivity and increase the chances of mistakes. Context switching is widespread in the software field. Sometimes, people work on various projects based on business needs. But whatever work you have committed, do one thing at a time. Time management is critical. Multitasking is usually NOT recommended as frequent switching across tasks reduces concentration, increases mistake probability, and eventually reduces productivity.

  While multitasking is sometimes unavoidable, effective planning can help to minimise its impact. For instance, a several years ago, I had to work on multiple projects simultaneously. I divided my work time into focused blocks to stay productive and aligned with my goals, dedicating two hours to each project. During those two hours, I concentrated entirely on one project, consciously resisting the temptation to think about the others. Such discipline helped me effectively contribute to multiple projects with good quality work. By effectively single-tasking within those time blocks, I was able to complete both projects efficiently and achieve my objectives. The concept of time-blocking is widely supported by productivity experts, including Cal Newport in his book *"Deep Work."*

Challenge 3 : Imposter Syndrome

Imposter Syndrome occurs when people doubt their success and abilities despite clear evidence of competence. They often feel that their achievements—whether degrees, honours, professional recognitions, awards, or praise—result from luck or external factors rather than their skills. They never truly feel their success; this persistent feeling of being a "fraud" can hold them back and cause significant stress.

My definition above is based on the original research article by psychologists *Pauline R. Clance and Suzanne A. Imes in 1978*, which studied high-achieving women. Since then, many studies have shown that imposter feelings are common among men and women across various fields. Based on my experience as a software professional, I have observed that imposter syndrome is common in software and technology careers. While it began with research focused on women, it is clear that anyone can experience it.

The term "Imposter Syndrome" was first introduced by psychologists Pauline R. Clance and Suzanne A. Imes in 1978, based on their study of high-achieving women. Since then, research has shown that imposter feelings affect both men and women across many fields. The observation about its presence in software and technology comes from my own professional experience.

Prerna, a senior QA analyst in a growing company, won spot recognition due to her bold performance on the project. A few of her teammates questioned her recognition, which made her wonder whether she got this award by fluke, although there was substantial evidence that her product test coverage was almost 100%.

Signs of Imposter Syndrome:

- **Overworking due to Self-Doubt** - You often work beyond your designated hours—not just out of dedication but to prove you're good enough. Deep down, you may feel that your success happened only because of that extra effort, not because of your talent or potential.

- **Fear of Expressing True Thoughts:** You often hesitate to express your fundamental ideas. Instead, you speak in a way that aligns with what others believe. Over time, you bury your voice out of fear of being judged or misunderstood. In doing so, you become trapped by others' opinions and hide your true potential.

- **Tagging success to likability:** You sometimes feel that your achievements are just because others like you—not because of your skills or effort. Deep down, you fear that if people honestly assessed your abilities, they might find you less capable than they thought.

- **Avoiding Confidence Out of Fear:** Even when you're capable and deserving, you avoid expressing your confidence or sharing your true views. You worry that others might expect more if you show what you know. This fear of rising expectations, or the possibility of failure, makes you hold back. So, you hide your real capabilities and talents—even though you have them.

This syndrome or feeling often causes:

a. Chronic stress and anxiety

b. Reduced Confidence

c. Hesitation to grab new opportunities

d. Overworking with self-doubt

e. Career Stagnation

f. Overworking and Burnout

g. Decreased Job satisfaction.

These internally cause missing new appealing opportunities within and outside organizations.

Do you want to be a victim of this syndrome? NO!!

<u>Counteractions to handle:</u>

Sharing your Experience: Share what you're experiencing with a trusted person—whether it's a mentor, colleague, friend, or peer or anyone. Many people go through this, and simply talking about the problem can ease the intensity. It can also offer fresh perspectives you might not have considered.

Reflective Exercise: Write down individuals that you feel tricked or bluffed. Analyse why do you feel so? Additionally, record positive feedback that you received, reflect on each of them. Identify why you discard them as "I am not fit to that".

Reframing Thoughts: When we write down our thoughts, if it is negative or limiting beliefs, we can convert into positive thoughts or powerful affirmations. For example: *"I think I might fail in the interview"*. This is limiting belief, now rephrase this to : *"I perform better in interview as I really prepared well."*

Pre-event self-doubt reduction: Self-doubt often arises before crucial events such as competitive exams, job interviews, presentations, or negotiation meetings. It is vital to recognize these feelings early and work to reduce self-doubt right before the event begins. When such thoughts emerge, pause and ask yourself:

"Do I have sufficient evidence to predict failure?"

Instead of giving in to doubt, cultivate empowering affirmations like:

"I have prepared thoroughly. I am capable and confident."

Additionally, practice visualizing success rather than focusing on potential failure. This mental rehearsal helps build confidence and reduces anxiety, improving overall performance.

Note: These signs, effects and counteractions to handle are adapted from observations first described by Clance and Imes (1978), with contextual interpretation for the software industry.

Celebrating even more minor accomplishments: Celebrating even the most minor accomplishments is one of the most powerful habits that can drive us toward our goals. When we handle complex projects, we move forward step by step. Every time we learn something new—like picking up a new programming language or solving a tricky bug—there's a quiet sense of satisfaction. We may not always show it, but it's there. I believe it's essential to pause and celebrate ourselves in those moments. It gives us the energy to keep going. *Research by Dr. Teresa Amabile supports this—she found that even small progress in meaningful work can significantly boost motivation and morale.*

Amabile, T. M., & Kramer, S. J. (2011). *The Progress Principle: Using Small Wins to Ignite Joy, Engagement, and Creativity at Work.* Harvard Business Review Press.

I've personally experienced this. In my younger days, even small wins were a big deal for me and my peers. We used to celebrate them together, and that joy kept us moving forward with more confidence.

Creating Positivity: You don't always need to be perfect; you only need to know whether you are progressing towards your goal. Realizing that learning everything is impossible, but knowing things around your domain is essential, so adhere to continuous learning.

Exercise: Now, identify all the obstacles you are facing right now that are stopping you from growing further. Using the above techniques, use appropriate methods for your problems.

	Common obstacles to your growth	Counteraction techniques
1		
2		
3		
4		
5		

Note: The data you will fill in counteraction techniques will become your next goal.

4.2 Strategies for Building Mental Toughness and Resilience

After recognizing the expected obstacles, we must become resilient, which comes with regular practice. Here, we can see what strategies we can follow to build a robust mental attitude and resilience.

1. Cultivating a growth mindset

As discussed earlier, embracing challenges as growth opportunities is key to developing a strong mindset. To recall, here are a few tips:

Accept Challenges: Think like this: there is nothing called failure; it is success or experience. Use your expertise to achieve success. Consider every challenge an opportunity to grow yourself and your organization. Also, it will add value to your experience. So, develop curiosity about your work.

Divert all criticisms to the learning path: Criticism is common in software. In software development, you can compare with code review comments. Pay attention to constructive criticism. Concentrate on the contents rather than how they say because everyone has different styles. Some suggestions mentioned in the criticism might add value to your work or experience, so grab that and work on it. It will help you to move towards a successful journey.

As an exercise, fill out the table below with the challenges you faced in your work and the lessons you learned.

	Challenges Faced	How you tackled	Lessons you learnt
1			
2			
3			
4			

Prioritize Focus Your Efforts Over the Outcomes:

Don't stress over the outcome. Instead, focus on putting your full effort in the right direction—especially in learning and problem-solving. In the long run, the effort you invest brings lasting satisfaction.

Journal your approaches, insights, and lessons learned. This simple habit will deepen your understanding and accelerate your growth.

2. Building Emotional Intelligence

According to Mental Health America (MHA),

"Emotional Intelligence (EI) is the ability to manage both your own emotions and understand the emotions of people around you. There are five key elements to EI:

- Self-awareness

- Self-regulation

- Motivation

- Empathy

- Social skills

People with high EI can identify how they are feeling, what those feelings mean, and how those emotions impact their behavior and, in turn, other people."

Mental Health America. (2025, February 27). What is emotional intelligence and how does it apply to the workplace? Mental Health America. Retrieved from: https://www.mhanational.org/learning-hub/what-is-emotional-intelligence-and-how-does-it-apply-to-the-workplace.

This article was originally available on an earlier Mental Health America URL prior to its February 27, 2025 publication date on the Learning Hub.

It is a crucial skill for teamwork and leadership because it helps build trust and collaboration through relationship and team interaction. In a corporate environment, emotional Intelligence involves being aware of how one's emotions affect one's behaviour and interactions with others and how the feelings of one's colleagues can impact workplace dynamics.

Jennifer, a project manager in a software company, noticed that her team member Jonathan, who was working on a high-priority issue, was sick and slightly shivering. Yet, he was working to address the customer-escalated problems. Jennifer exhibited "*self-awareness*" by understanding his situation; she remained calm as she forecasted the risk associated with the project. There, she showed "*self-regulation*". By displaying "*social skills* ", she immediately stepped into Jonathan to check what happened and said: "*Are you okay? It seems you are out of your health, so it's probably time to take sick time.*" She added, "*Don't worry about the escalation issue; I will delegate to someone else*". Thereby, she exhibited "*empathy*". And finally, she said – "*you can do better once you recover*". Here, she motivated him for future work.

Here, Jennifer exhibited all stages of emotional Intelligence (EI). She understood the team member's health, quickly restated him, and delegated the work to other team members. In this way, she could balance her emotions of handling pressure to complete tasks and the emotions of other team members.

Improving emotional Intelligence involves:

- Be aware of your emotions and understand how they affect your behaviour.

- Control your reactions, especially during stressful conditions

- Develop empathy and respond appropriately

Improving your emotional Intelligence can create a positive environment where people understand and support you.

As an exercise, fill the table below with details about how you have exhibited Emotional Intelligence in various scenarios.

SI	Scenarios	Exhibited emotional Intelligence: Yes/No?	Yes -> Say thank you to yourself No -> Write down what stopped you from doing so.	Write corrective actions for how you could exhibit emotional Intelligence next time when a similar situation occurs.
1				
2				
3				
4				
5				

3. Developing Positive thinking and Mental toughness

We face many failures during software development during our experiments and sometimes approaches. It is essential to think positively and stay strong to proceed further. While learning, it is also necessary to reframe our negative thoughts to proceed with growth. The next question is, how?

As mentioned above, negative thoughts are common when dealing with complex projects. The primary thing is replacing those negative thoughts and false beliefs with positive thoughts that push you towards success.

Cognitive reframing is a powerful psychological tool commonly used to address self-doubt, fear of failure, and imposter syndrome. The technique rooted in Cognitive Behavioural Therapy (CBT) helps individuals shift negative thinking patterns into more constructive perspectives.

Dr. Aaron T. Beck originally introduced cognitive reframing in his ground-breaking book Cognitive Therapy and Emotional Disorders. It was later expanded by Dr. Albert Ellis through his work in Rational Emotive Behavior Therapy (REBT), exceptionally detailed in A Guide to Rational Living.

Reframing thoughts often involves transforming *negative thinking* into *positive thinking*. When you encounter any failure in any personal or professional life, treat the situation as an experience and note down the learnings. Never degrade yourself in such a situation. Make sure NOT to repeat the same mistakes in the following days by exhibiting self-awareness and taking corrective actions. It emphasizes *pushing beyond our comfort zone and staying resilient to work towards growth and success.* So if any setbacks happen in the office work, be resilient and work towards growth and success.

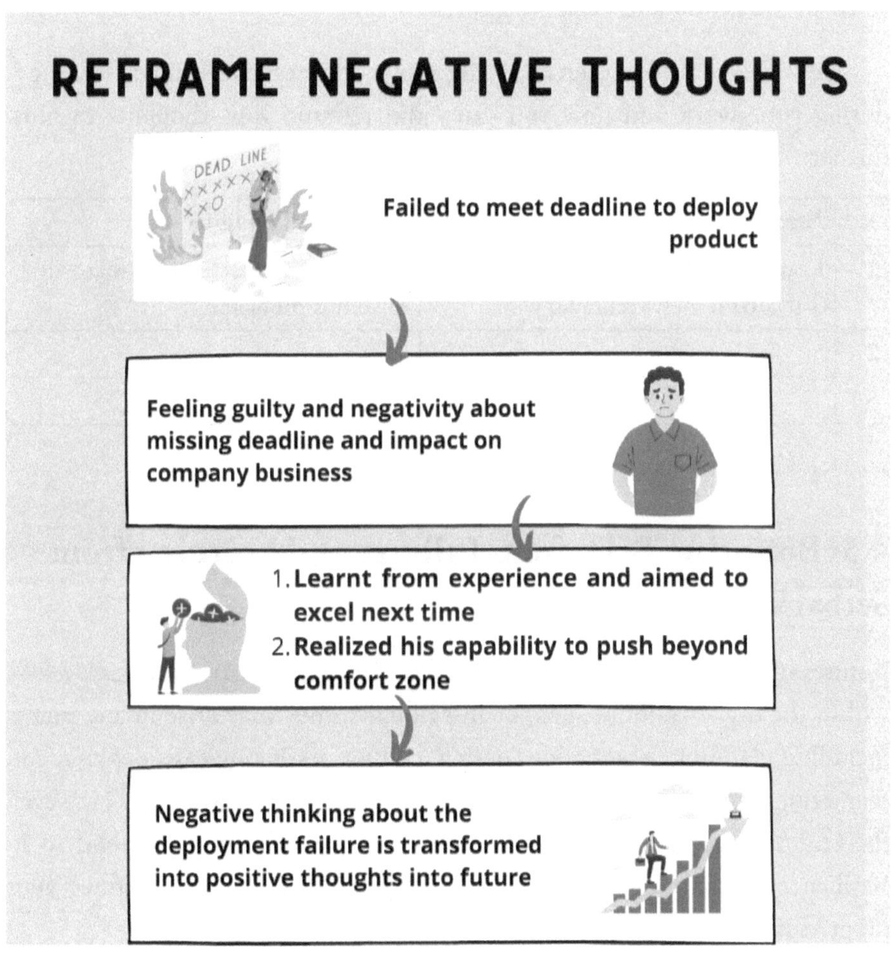

Figure 4.2: Reframe Negative Thoughts

Henry, a DevOps engineer working in a CMM-level company, once failed to meet the product deployment deadlines. Initially, he felt frustrated and pessimistic about missing the schedule. But after learning about the power of *cognitive reframing*, he began to look at the situation differently.

He told himself: *"Though I missed the deadline, I've gained valuable insights and experiences. These learnings will help me to handle future deployments more efficiently. I'm grateful that stepping beyond my comfort zone has opened new doors for growth."* This shift in mindset transformed his negative thoughts into constructive action and personal growth.

Now it is time for exercise; write down the negative thoughts you got during your work and how you can / did reframe your thoughts to grow further:

	Negative Thoughts	**Cognitive Thoughts**
1	I can't solve this problem because it is related to new technology.	I will learn the technology that will solve this problem.
2		
3		
4		

4.3 Bouncing Back from Failures and Learning from Setbacks

Failures are a natural part of the software world and can occur at various levels—within the organization, teams, or individuals. They may arise in any phase, including planning, negotiation, design, coding, testing, release, deployment, marketing, accounting, human resources, or facilities management. However, the critical factor is not the failure itself but your ability to respond to it. Resilience—how you recover, learn, and grow from failure—defines your progress and success.

In the following section, let's explore practical strategies to face failures and assess them as stepping stones for success. Let's explore how to transform failures into learning and development opportunities.

1. Embrace failure as an opportunity to learn

We have discussed this multiple times before. If you already know it, please skip this section(5.3.1). You must treat failure as a stepping stone to success and an opportunity to learn. Every failure opens a door to experience. You must expect failure while doing great things, learn from it, and move forward.

How can I learn from failure? As discussed in Chapter 3, section 3.3, conduct a retrospective for yourself. As yourself:

    a.   What went wrong? Is it my procrastination, or is the topic complex?

    b.   External disturbances? Internal disturbances? Health issue?

Ask yourselves the maximum number of questions and find prompt answers. Take actions based on your answers, set goals and work on achieving them.

2. Decoupling sense of self from Outcome

Have you ever wondered who the most important person on this planet? Its **"you"**. Its not about selfishness but self-care. Without taking care of ourself – physically, mentally and emotionally, we can't support others or live our purpose. I've learned this through moments of struggle—only I can truly nurture myself. The Bhagavad Gita emphasizes this idea through:

One should focus on elevating self and never degrade oneself.

– Chapter 6, Verse 5 (6.5)

So we should not make ourself down in whatever the situation- professionally, socially or personally.

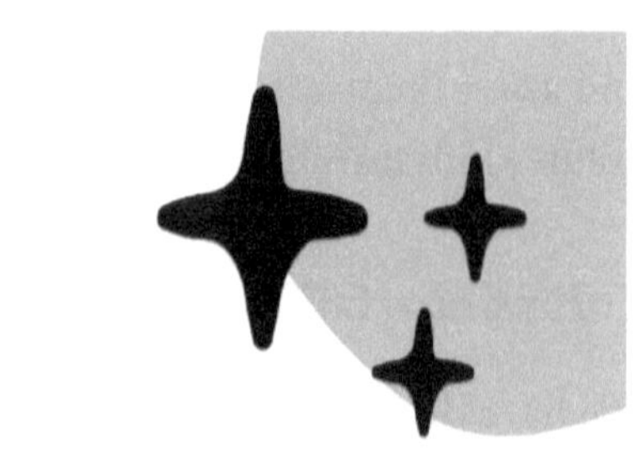

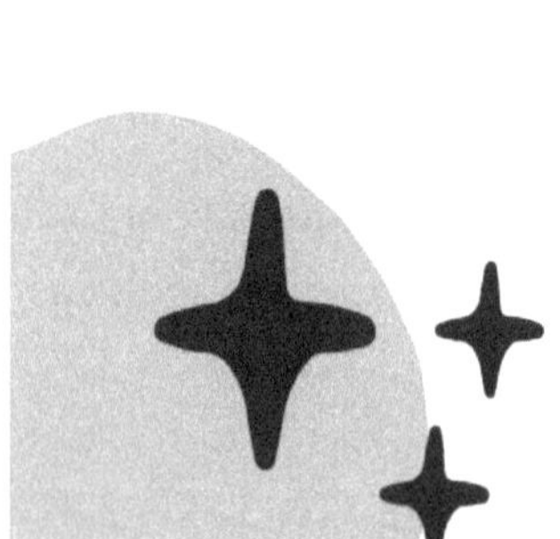

Figure 5.3: The Power of Self

Respecting and showing kindness to family members, relatives, friends, and everyone in society are natural. It's also essential to respect and treat yourself as one of them.

Never blame yourself if you make any mistakes in your projects or while making decisions. Instead, tell yourself, "*I am not the first person who made this mistake. Everyone would have experienced self-doubts and exhibit fear of failure at some point in their lives. It's okay as I made a mistake, but I learned a lesson from this incident; I will apply this knowledge next time so that I will not repeat such mistakes and will head towards success.*"

Practising self-compassion will help to build more resilience and a balanced mindset. Here are some techniques for self-compassion:

Technique	Data	Action
Self-Compassion Journal	Write down few struggles which you faced in the day. How could you help your friend if they faces similar situation? Apply the same thing to you.	1. 2. 3.
Self-Compassion Break	Acknowledge difficulties in the work, speak kindly to yourself, take breaks, come up with new ideas to tackle the listed challenges and continue to work	1. 2. 3. 4. 5. 6.
Write a compassionate letter on yourself	Write a letter to yourself as if your close friend is writing to you, which includes support and encouragement that you can get from others when you are down.	Write a letter in few sentences OR you can use extra paper to do so.
Forgiveness	Identify if you have any regret about anything and practice forgiving yourself. Write down regrets, reflect on them and forgive yourself	1. 2. 3. 4. 5. 6.

The practices shared in this section—such as keeping a Self-Compassion Journal, taking a Self-Compassion Break, writing compassionate letters to oneself, and nurturing forgiveness—are inspired by the pioneering work of Dr Kristin Neff and Dr Christopher Germer, co-founders of the Mindful Self-Compassion (MSCO) program. Their insights are drawn from decades of research. They are thoughtfully presented in their published works, including Dr Neff's book on the science and practice of self-kindness, Dr Germer's guide to blending mindfulness with emotional healing, and their co-authored workbook that offers practical exercises to build self-compassion in daily life.

I am also grateful to my mind performance coach, Dr. Manjunath, who personally introduced practicing similar techniques (for the concepts mentioned in this section) in his workshop and has been a constant support in my growth journey.

Summary (Mindmap)

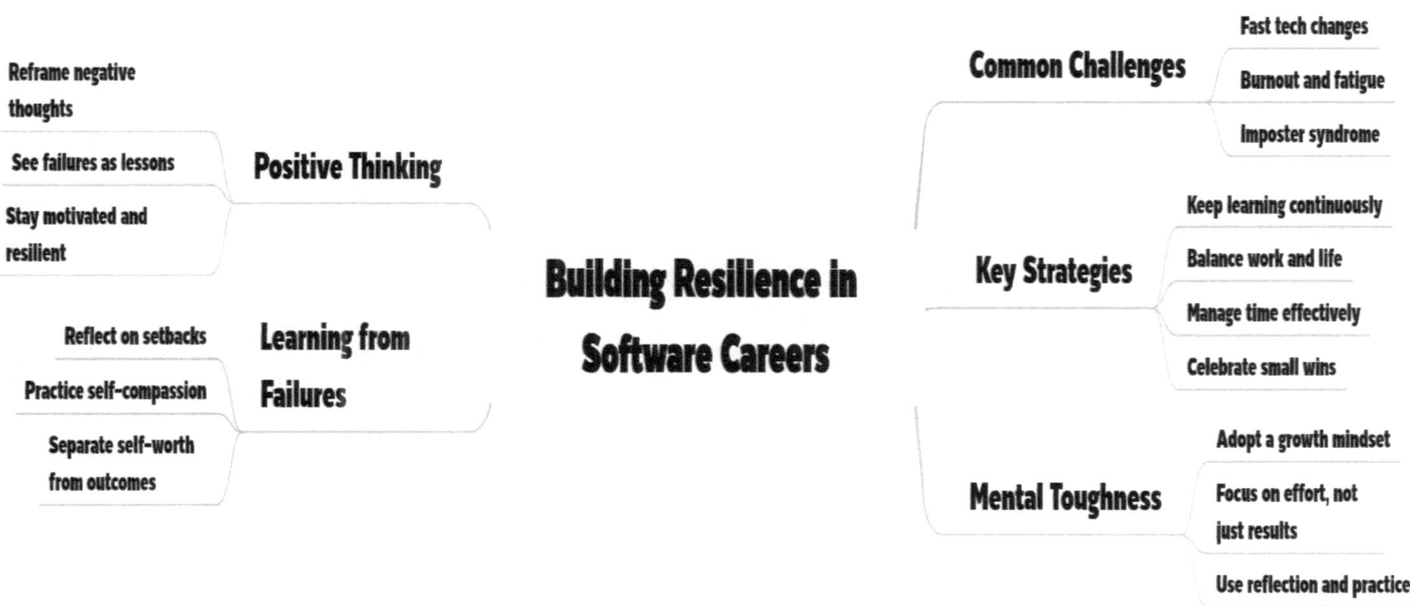

Chapter 5

The Web of Opportunity: Interlacing Connections for Career Advancement

"Alone we can do so little; together we can do so much."

– Helen Keller, *Optimism: An Essay,* 1903

Have you ever wondered what the crucial factor is in career advancement? What else is required to excel in your professional life besides your domain strength?

The answer is PROFESSIONAL NETWORKING.

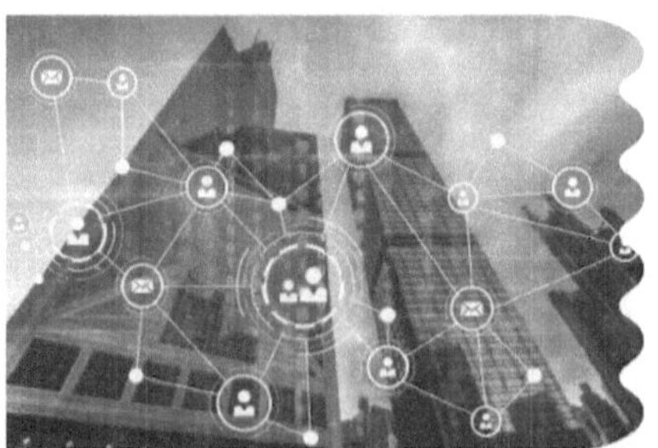

Figure 5.1: Professional Networking

Along with technical skills, strong networking support and good collaboration skills are necessary to succeed in the software world. Collaboration is vital for success in this industry, as different organizations collaborate to create system(s). For instance, some companies work on mobile phones, while others elaborate on mobile network systems to form 5G ecosystems, revolutionising voice and video quality.

Collaborations will occur in regular office work, where human resource teams, product development teams, QA teams, Agile teams, IT teams, innovation teams, support teams, and others will work together to run an organization successfully.

So, we need a good network to achieve success in our organizations. The chapter "Building Your Network: Collaborating for Success" describes the importance of building a network in IT. It is broadly categorized into three sections. Section 5.1 explains the power of collaboration and how it helps develop professional relationships. Section 5.2 explains effective networking strategies for software professionals to build networking— section 5.3 deals with how to seek effective mentorship in the software field.

5.1 The Power of Collaboration: Uplifting the Professional Relationships

a) Have you ever thought about why collaboration matters in the IT world?

I have observed that new employees often work together on specific tasks. Sometimes, collaboration is essential for maintaining compatibility across the team(s) when projects require integrating multiple functionalities. Collaborative projects enable team members to share knowledge, learn from each other, and combine their strengths to solve problems. They increase productivity and improve human relationships and, thereby, professional networking. So, be happy while working with a group or a team.

In any organisation, teamwork is vital for success! Collaboration is crucial, whether forming a new team, creating and testing new products, or coordinating between HR and Finance during employee transitions. There are countless opportunities for different groups to work together, making the possibilities for success endless!

b) Collaboration is often required for :

Solving complex problems: Collaboration becomes essential when solving complex problems. For example, imagine a software product developed by Company X. A customer reports an outage issue occurring in the field. The customer support team collects and reports all the details to the development team. Since multiple teams are responsible for different product parts, each team must analyze the issue from their perspective.

Finally, the problem is narrowed down to a specific module owned by a team where a deadlock occurs in a code. A talented engineer identifies the root cause and provides a fix. The testing team validates the changes, and the development operations team ships the fix to the customer.

This example shows how collaboration across various organizational teams is crucial to solving complex issues effectively.

Innovations: Sometimes, novel solutions emerge when creative ideas are combined with expertise from diverse fields.

The mobile phone is a classic example of this. Its evolution brought together professionals from hardware engineering, chipset design, operating systems, app development, and telecom networks—all contributing to the powerful devices we now carry in our pockets.

Knowledge Sharing: Every software professional is skilled in one or more areas, but it's impossible for a single person to master everything. That's why team members need to share their knowledge. When people share what they know, it helps others understand the product better.

In software companies, new joiners are usually trained by experts from different domains so they can quickly understand how the product works.

Project productivity: Collaboration across different teams often drives large projects forward. Each team focuses on a different part of the product simultaneously, which helps speed up development and boosts overall productivity.

Exercise:

	Project name or Team name	Did you use any innovative solutions?	Did you learn anything during collaborative work? Yes/No If yes, journal here	Did you gain knowledge from your teammates? (Yes/ No) If yes, journal here	Did you share your knowledge or experience with your teammates? (Yes/ No) If yes, journal here
1					
2					
3					
4					
5					

Revisiting the above table could help to reuse solutions documented here in different places.

c) Building collaborative Professional relationship

Maintaining good professional relationships with every person you interact with daily in your work environment is essential. It will make you feel good and help you progress your work faster. A good professional always proactively contacts colleagues and develops a pleasant rapport as much as they can. Relationships can be improved by active listening, showing empathy, and open communication.

Here are a few techniques that help in building solid collaborations:

Be Open to feedback: Feedback is essential for self-development in the work environment. You can get feedback from co-workers, mentors, managers, architects, leads or anyone. Whenever you interact with someone, be a good listener and, if possible, be open to giving thoughtful, constructive, and respectful feedback. It will create a healthy collaborative environment where individuals feel respected and valued.

Several years back, while working on a networking project, I needed help understanding the technicality behind the code. One of my colleagues carefully listened to my words and suggested going through specific RFCs to get the roots of the code I was going through. In turn, I thanked him, as I felt valued and heard.

Exhibit Proactiveness: Proactiveness is very important in the software field, irrespective of domain, position, or experience. It will help with productivity and winning the confidence of your peers or supervisors. This behaviour will also help to achieve collaborations.

Whenever you notice your colleagues struggling in a project scenario, and if you know or have expertise in that skill, be proactive and help them overcome the problems. It will be helpful for the team and help improve professional relationships.

Communicate Transparently: Communication plays a unique role in collaboration and building strong relationships. You must communicate concisely and carefully when working on complex projects and presenting your thoughts. Smiling during communication will add value. Proper communication will help you participate actively in collaborative work and build rapport with colleagues. Also, while showing empathy, communicate thoughtfully. It will help you gain confidence and make a good relationship.

Learn to Appreciate: Whatever your position or experience level, whenever someone offers great help that adds value to your work, make sure to appreciate them. Whether that person is your reporter, supervisor, teammate, people from other groups, or anyone you deal with regularly, show gratitude for their work. It will help build good professional relationships.

Some of the ideas shared in this section—like taking initiative, being a good listener, and building mutual respect—are closely related to the principles explained in Stephen R. Covey's The 7 Habits of Highly Effective People. That book highlights habits such as being proactive, seeking to understand others, and creating win-win situations—all of which can be powerful tools for building strong and meaningful professional relationships.

As an exercise, kindly fill in the data below:

Technique	Questions	Yes or No	If No, ask yourself why and what corrective action is.
Be Open to Feedback	Do you actively listen during interactions like meetings or discussions?		
	Did you provide thoughtful, constructive, and respectful feedback when needed for the project?		
	Did you show gratitude for the feedback you received to create a healthy environment.?		
Exhibit Proactiveness	Did you identify and assist colleagues struggling with tasks for which you have expertise?		
	Did you anticipate potential project challenges and take steps to address them early?		
	Have you volunteered for tasks or initiatives that require additional effort to benefit the team or organization?		

	Are you Sharing resources or knowledge proactively to enhance team efficiency?		
Communicate Transparently	Are you Communicating ideas clearly and concisely, particularly in complex scenarios?		
	Are you smiling and maintaining positive body language during discussions to foster trust?		
	Are you showing empathy through thoughtful communication, especially during challenging conversations?		
	Do you regularly check in with colleagues to ensure task alignment and clarity?		
Learn to Appreciate	Do you verbally acknowledge the contributions of peers, supervisors, or team members?		
	Did you send thank-you notes or emails for significant assistance or support?		
	Did you highlight team members' efforts during meetings or presentations?		
	Are you celebrating small wins together to strengthen relationships and boost morale?		

5.2 Effective Strategies for Building Networking - Software Professionals

Network building is one of the essential skills every software professional needs to develop. It is not just about meeting people and greeting them. But it is about exchanging thoughts and ideas, learning new skills, mentoring, helping each other with new opportunities, and mutually meaningful and friendly relationships. We can do professional networking within and outside organizations. Applications like LinkedIn help get in touch with people from the same and different organizations. If you still need to create a social media profile like LinkedIn, please make it immediately and build your network.

Now let's see a little bit more detail about networking:

What makes you think networking is important?

Growth and Learning Opportunities:

Let me explain how networking has helped me:

Through networking, I've been able to learn and grow in many ways:

- I stay updated on emerging market trends and new technologies, as many professionals share their experiences and insights on platforms like LinkedIn.

- I noticed some professionals often share articles from their domain expertise that offer valuable real-world insights.

- I often receive links to valuable learning resources and training opportunities.

- Professionals from HR backgrounds regularly share helpful tips on soft skills, work-life balance, and career development.

- I also help others by sharing my experiences and technical skills.

- Most importantly, networking is helping me explore new career opportunities and stay aware of what's happening in the job market.

- Reading such content and interacting with others helps me stay current with modern technologies and gives me direction for my future goals. It's been a big boost for my career.

Knowing about such articles help you to updated on modern technologies and guide you on your future goals to propel your career.

Support and Guidelines:

Depending on your situation, you can leverage your network support and here are some of them:

- **Exploring career paths:** You can contact people in your network for diverse perspectives and advice when making career decisions.

- **Clarifying technical questions:** If you're stuck or curious about a specific technology, someone in your network might already have the answers or experience you're looking for.

- **Job transitions:** If you've been laid off or are seeking new opportunities, you can (with discretion) post within your network for leads and support.

- **Hiring Help:** When hiring for your team, sharing a clear and detailed job description within your professional network can help attract well-suited and qualified candidates.

- **LinkedIn recommendations:** You can request endorsements or recommendations from current or former colleagues to strengthen your profile. But ensure you build a good professional relationship with them before your request.

- **Referrals for job openings:** Your network can connect you with people hiring or refer you for roles that align with your expertise.

Seeking new opportunities:

If you are looking for new job opportunities, networking will be beneficial. Create your profile and update all your skillsets. Make sure you use those skills that you are comfortable with. We can't predict when we will get into a crisis, so be always ready like a professional soldier to face interviews. You can also browse jobs that interest you and apply for them. Except for my first organization, all my previous company interviews happened after applying for jobs on LinkedIn.

Build your brand:

If you want to build a professional brand, you need to network. You can attend tech conferences, contribute to open-source projects, and give presentations on areas of interest that will strengthen your brand.

Networking Strategies

a. **Leverage Online platforms:** You can build and develop networking by creating profiles on online platforms like LinkedIn and adding the folks you know directly or indirectly to your network. It may be your previous company colleagues, classmates, HRs, entrepreneurs, and anyone you know through any means. LinkedIn is a typical example of building a professional network.

b. **Contributing to open source projects:** Have you ever participated in an open source project, such as Linux? If not, I recommend you start today itself. Participating in open-source projects helps build your knowledge and a strong network. You can also get mentorship from people from such projects, and it is beneficial for collaborating with others on such projects.

c. **Join Professional Communities:** If we want to expand our professional community or join existing forums, online platforms like GitHub, Stack Overflow, GoogleForums, etc., will play a crucial role. With that, there is a high chance of expanding the network, skills, and opportunities. These platforms help to clarify the questions or doubts that arise during live projects. Additionally, if you are facing any trouble with your project(tools, programming languages, API usage, etc), you can seek help from such communities.

d. **Attend Industry events and conferences:** Many organizations conduct industry events often. It would help if you considered attending such events because they are essential for learning about upcoming software industry trends. They will also help you build a robust professional network by allowing you to meet professionals from different organizations. So start exploring such events and join when you get a chance.

Let's do an exercise in your case:

Key Aspect	Questions	Yes or No	If no, ask yourself why and what corrective action is needed. Write down your action item here.
Networking Importance	Have you created your LinkedIn Profile? Are you regularly updating it with relevant skills and experience?		
	Have you engaged with peers by exchanging thoughts, sharing insights, and mentoring others?		
	Have you built decent professional relationships within and outside your organization?		
	Are you staying informed about trends, technologies, and industry practices through your network?		
Growth and Learning	Are you following individuals who share technical articles or real-world experiences?		
	Are you sharing your expertise through posts, articles, or discussions?		

	Are you leveraging your network to stay updated on marketing trends and technical advancements?		
	Are you seeking insights into work-life balance and soft skills from HR professionals in your network?		
Support and Guidelines	Are you seeking advice on career paths, technology-specific questions, or hiring needs within your network?		
	Are you posting your resume cautiously when seeking job opportunities or recommendations?		
	Are you offering peer support by providing feedback or sharing your insights?		
Seeking Opportunities	Are you updating your professional profile on your core skills?		
	Are you using LinkedIn or a similar job portal to browse and apply for jobs matching your expertise during crises?		
	Are you always interview-ready by maintaining a professional skillset?		
Building Your Brand	Are you attending tech conferences and industry events to build credibility and expand your network?		

	Are you contributing to open-source projects to showcase expertise and collaborate with global professionals?		
	Do you deliver presentations or talks on areas of interest to establish thought leadership?		
Networking Strategies	Have you built your network on LinkedIn by connecting with colleagues, HRs, and entrepreneurs?		
	Have you participated in open-source projects for mentorship and collaboration?		
	Are you Engaging with professional communities like GitHub, Stack Overflow, and similar platforms?		
	Are you attending industry events to learn about trends and meet professionals from various organizations?		

5.3 Mentorship in Software World: Finding Guides for Your Journey

Mentorship empowers individuals to think critically and solve problems independently. In the software industry, mentoring and inspiring others are vital in acquiring essential knowledge and advancing careers. They also improve leadership and communication skills.

Figure 5.2: Mentorship

Mentorship is necessary for everyone in the software world because no one is considered a *"perfect software professional."* Even company CEOs often have mentors, either directly or indirectly. This section focuses on the importance of mentorship, inspiring through personal experiences, building trust and rapport, and providing constructive feedback. Let's start.

Why do we need Mentors?

Mentorship is essential for everyone in the software world who starts new tasks. It offers incredible benefits by providing an opportunity to share valuable knowledge and educating mentees with crucial tools, processes, project details, and a problem-solving approach. It prepares individuals to meet business needs and professional goals, eventually contributing to growth and success.

The goal of mentorship is not to provide spoon-feeding but to empower mentors to address business needs independently and push them to gain expertise in different business areas. A good mentor will encourage mentors to learn and take complete ownership of certain functions independently.

When the mentor approaches the mentee for an answer, the mentor will ask guiding questions like, "*Out of the several approaches you proposed, what solution is better and why?*" It will give the mentee confidence, and the mentee will start believing their own decisions.

Building Trust and Rapport between mentor and mentee

Building trust is required for successful mentorship or outstanding leadership. Mentees should be confident in their mentors when expressing their thoughts or doing new experiments. There should be rapport between members and the leader, which is helpful for better learning, excellent team collaboration, and good human relationships, which helps build professional networking.

Both trust and rapport will not come in a single day; they take time, depending on actions, approaches, kindness, communication, honesty, and empathy. Show empathy and a positive attitude towards your work and those around you. It will also reflect on you. Over time, trust and good rapport will also build, making you feel comfortable in your work environment.

I experienced one of my (senior and) mentors in one organization becoming a colleague in another. We had an excellent rapport and felt good working together again in the new company. So, develop a good rapport, whether you are a mentor or mentee.

Exercise:

	Questions	YES or NO	If NO, corrective action
1	Can you show empathy and a positive attitude in all interactions with colleagues?		
2	Are you able to communicate honestly and openly with team members?		
3	Will you be consistent in actions to build credibility over time?		

| 4 | Did you focus on ethical behaviour to gain respect and trust? | | |
| 5 | Are you able to build friendly, professional relationships to foster collaboration? | | |

Inspiring Through Personal Experiences

Another powerful way to mentor and inspire others is by sharing our experiences. Talking about challenges you faced in your earlier experiences and mistakes you made will humanize growth and learning. It can motivate mentees, as others are facing such difficulties.

Janhavi, a technical lead mentoring Vishwas, a junior engineer, talking to him: "*When I started the project, I saw a nightmare, especially while debugging complex issues with GDB, but after a series of experiments, I was able to narrow down the problem by step by step procedure and eventually solved the same. I believe you are also in a similar stage where I was; I think you will also get through this* ". Such words motivate the mentees, who realize that such challenges are typical in the software field and are part of learning. Here, Janhavi inspired Vishwas by sharing her own experience.

Exercise:

	Questions	YES or NO	Description
1	Can you share your challenges and explain how you overcame them?		
2	Can your past experiences relate to the current situations of your mentees?		
3	List down to illustrate that mistakes are part of the learning process to motivate others.		

Giving Constructive Feedback

We have discussed the importance of feedback several times earlier.

Giving constructive feedback from mentors or leaders will positively impact team members. They should show resistance to their mistakes but concentrate on how to correct them. Help them understand the areas of improvement and provide actionable steps to fix them.

Here is an example. Nelson, a junior developer in a software company, submits a piece of code that needs to be reviewed. Jonathan, a mentor, says, "This code works, but it could be optimized. But let's use Standard Template Library(C++) to store and retrieve data. " This type of feedback helps Nelson's improvement and boosts his confidence. Avoid negative facial expressions like furious, disappointment, complaining, surprise, etc., which might make members feel down and discouraged, affecting their work.

Exercise:

	Questions	YES or NO	Description
1	Can you focus on solutions and areas for improvement in feedback?		
2	Can you provide actionable steps to help the team member grow?		
3	Can you use positive and encouraging language during discussions?		
4	Can you avoid negative facial expressions or tones to maintain motivation?		

Empowering Others to Take Ownership

Never micromanage. It frustrates team members and prevents them from getting the desired results on time. It also creates a toxic work atmosphere, hampering productivity.

As a leader or mentor, you can empower others to own their work. People who feel trusted and empowered are likelier to take initiative and contribute in style.

For example, you can say, "*I trust you can handle this part of the product. If you stuck somewhere, I'm there to help, but I am confident you can do it.*" It encourages autonomy and helps team members develop their proactiveness and problem-solving skills.

Exercise:

	Questions	YES or NO	Description
1	Can you delegate tasks clearly and express confidence in your team's abilities ?		
2	Can you avoid micromanaging and give space for independent problem-solving?		
3	Will you be available to support but let the team take the lead?		
4	You often say encouraging words such as: "I trust you to handle this?"		

Summary

The chapter emphasizes the importance of professional networking and collaboration for individual success in the software world. To thrive in the industry along with technical skills, professionals need the following skills:

- good networking

- collaboration

The Collaboration Power

Collaboration has become an integral part of the:

- Solving complex problems

- Sharing knowledge

- Innovation

Collaboration helps to increase the overall productivity of a team, group, or organisation.

Additionally, it highlights how collaboration uniquely plays a role in complex projects:

- to achieve massive results

- improve professional relationships.

Further factors that enhance cooperation and build trust among colleagues are:

- Active listening

- Open communication,

- Empathy, and

- Constructive feedback

Effective Networking Strategies

Networking strategies involve:

- building meaningful relationships,

- sharing knowledge,

- seeking growth opportunities.

The following factors help professionals to build robust networks they can leverage when needed:

- Platforms like LinkedIn,

- Participation in open-source projects

- Attending industry events.

Networking supports career growth, personal branding, and access to new opportunities.

Mentorship in Tech

Mentorship fosters critical thinking and independent problem-solving. It is associated with the following skills to help mentees achieve professional goals:

- building trust or rapport,

- sharing personal experiences and

- offering constructive feedback

Effective mentorship empowers individuals to take ownership of their roles, develop confidence, and grow professionally.

Chapter 6

The Learning River: Flowing with Change in the Tech Landscape

"Nahi Jnanena Sadrusham"

– Bhagavad Gita, Chapter 4, Verse 38

Translation: "There is nothing as purifying as knowledge."

It translates to nothing equal to knowledge and highlights the importance of having knowledge, which we can obtain through continuous learning.

In software development, we use the term loop to refer to repeating specific steps until we meet certain conditions. A continuous loop is a never-ending loop, so a constant learning loop means learning should never end.

When a software professional stops learning, that person is steering towards career decline. Continuous learning should be a mantra of any software professional, irrespective of their position, organisation, country, place, or experience. We can compare technologies like a river. Most of the time, new technologies supersede old ones, which has become a never-ending process in the last few decades. With revolutions in the cloud and artificial Intelligence, the trends will continue for a few more decades.

Continuous learning helps you stay ahead in tech and builds your confidence. The chapter "Continuous Learning Loop: Staying Ahead in Tech" is divided into three sections: Section **1:** Embracing Lifelong Learning in Software Life, Section 2: Exploring various learning opportunities, and Section 3: Emphasizing Continuous Feedback for Growth.

6.1 Embracing Lifelong Learning in Software Life

With advancements in inventions and innovations, technology is progressing in multiple dimensions. Most organizations with a growth vision are moving towards building new products while still keeping legacy products to generate revenue until the end of the product's life.

Working on modern technologies, processes, methodologies, and innovations becomes essential for every software professional. The technologies we had a few decades back differ from today's. The invention of new programming languages, frameworks, enhancements on O.S. flavours, and a variety of other things have helped everyone upgrade themselves to stay competent, i.e., software life. At the micro level, we need to save our jobs. So, learning is a never-ending process for software professionals(everyone who works in a software company, not limited to software developers).

Why lifelong learning?

Learning will continue with formal education or experience with some organizations. It needs to come along with your professional life. It might make some people uncomfortable, but you have decided to thrive in this industry. The bright side of learning is that not only will you gain knowledge, but it also builds your legacy and identity. You will stand distinguished!!

According to the *Johari Window model* by Joseph Luft and Harrington Ingham(1955), there are four quadrants for learning.

Q1: "open area" -> known to you and others	Q2: "blind area" -> unknown to you and known to others
Q3: "hidden area" -> known to you and unknown to others	Q4: "unknown area" -> unknown to you and unknown to others

We can apply this to learning methods as below:

You can apply technology when you and your colleagues know about it daily.

When you realize you don't know, and colleagues know technologies, start working on learning things or getting help from that person to understand better. When you realize you know the technology and colleagues don't know it, do knowledge sharing if they like. Practice continuous learning when you and your colleagues don't know certain technologies.

A Sanskrit proverb I learned during high school says: "*Vidwan Savatra Poojyathe,*" which translates to "*a learnt man respected everywhere.*" You will automatically gain respect for your knowledge, whether in your office life or outside. Your projects, employer, and clients will benefit from your learning. I have experienced that learning will instigate your curiosity, help you think in different directions, improve your creativity and adaptability, and make you resilient.

Your knowledge and skills will make your employer think twice before touching you, even during the recession.

So what are you waiting for?

What strategies do you need to follow for continuous learning?

If you need to adopt lifelong learning(in fact, you have to), attitude and mindset matter a lot. Develop growth or dynamic mindset strategies, which were discussed in earlier chapters. Of course, you will encounter a lot of hurdles initially; it might be your procrastination, professional and personal workload, or any other factors specific to individuals. You need to remember and tune your mind that if I need to survive, I must learn continuously by pushing myself. After overcoming initial problems, you will enjoy the process. Let's see the strategies we can use:

Set learning goals: We have seen this multiple times before. Establish Doran's S.M.A.R.T. (Specific, Measurable, Achievable, Relevant, and Time-Bound) framework goals for your learning and projects. (we discussed this concept several times earlier).

Create a learning Schedule: Dedicate time each day for focused learning. As mentioned in chapter Consider using the *Pomodoro Technique*—a time management method developed by *Francesco Cirillo*—which involves working in focused intervals (typically 25–40 minutes) followed by short breaks. For example, you might work for 40 minutes and take a 5-minute break. Tracking your learning and applying retrospective reviews (as discussed in earlier chapters), helps you adapt and refine your short-term goals effectively.

Develop curiosity: You must become more curious to learn and explore new technologies.

Seek and accept constructive feedback: Feedback is necessary to correct ourselves and push ourselves in the right direction. Accept constructive feedback promptly and work on it. Seek your mentors to check if you are on the right path in your learning.

Test your knowledge by doing smaller projects if you can afford it.

Exercise:

	Questions	YES or NO	If NO, make a plan to do so.
1	Can you create Doran's S.M.A.R.T. (Specific, Measurable, Achievable, Relevant, Time-Bound) learning goals?		
2	Can you dedicate a fixed time daily for learning?		
3	Are you using the Pomodoro technique: 40 minutes of focus, 5-minute break.?		
4	Can you track your progress and use retrospectives to adjust short-term goals?		
5	Are you able to explore new technologies and trends?		
6	Can you read industry blogs, attend webinars, or watch tutorials?		
7	Can you regularly request feedback from mentors or peers?		

8	Are you actively working on suggestions and corrections?		
9	Can you learn concepts by working on smaller, manageable projects?		

6.2 Identifying Learning Opportunities: Courses, Conferences, and Communities

Once you set your goals, it is time to look for the resources to learn. In the case of Software developers, they often refer to their products' documentation, such as development manuals, specifications, RFCs, design documentation, open source specifications, technical blogs, YouTube videos(sometimes), git hubs, stack overflows, Reddits, Google forums, and even their company forums, to learn new things. Sometimes, they experiment in their working environment to understand better. Similar things can apply to other areas as well.

These practices are well-recognized in the software development community.

Exercises:

Here are some of the learning opportunities:

1	Many organizations will conduct internal training during the joining process or new project requirements. So, please make use of it 100% without procrastinating.
2	Many software professionals use online platforms such as Udemy, Coursera, LinkedIn Learning, YouTube(to some extent), Udacity, Edx, etc. Udemy seems the cheapest and my favourite one. You will get to do a project with some of the courses.
3	Tech conferences—such as AWS re: Invent, Google I/O, or Microsoft Build—offer hands-on exposure to emerging tools, expert sessions, and networking opportunities

4	As widely discussed in the developer community, active participation in online forums like Stack Overflow, Reddit, and GitHub fosters learning and contribution.
5	Reading books is another way to enhance your skills on topics of concern, offline or online.
6	Obtaining Online certifications is one of the best ways to gain expertise on a specific topic. It depends on your domain or the area you want to pursue. For example AWS (developer, solution architect, etc.), AZURE, Google Cloud, A.I., Python, networking, soft skills, etc.
7	You can also learn from peers, mentors, managers, architects, other teams, or friends.
8	Contributions to open-source projects are another way of learning.

By exploring these, you can increase your learning skills.

6.3 Implementing Feedback Loops: Leveraging Input for Growth

Self-review is undoubtedly essential, but it may not be sufficient. Sometimes, we overlook our mistakes. It makes feedback from others valuable. Regular feedback and reviews are necessary in software development to avoid issues early and improve quality. Consistent input from mentors or peers sharpens your work, boosts your confidence, and helps you handle self-doubt or imposter feelings. From my experience, reviewing different areas like requirements, architecture, design, code, unit tests, DevOps practices, YAML files, scripts, and test cases has helped reduce rework and made the overall output much more reliable.

Mentoring is essential for any software professional, especially when dealing with unfamiliar technologies, and it requires help to follow the proper path. You need help when you get stuck several times and to learn essential things to excel in the project.

I am so lucky to have had great mentors from day one of my career and across different organizations. If you were my mentor and you are reading this book, it's all because of your help that I reached this stage of writing this book. From the bottom of my heart, I am saying thank you.

So, feedback is essential for anyone to grow and excel in the software industry.

We call feedback a loop because whenever you implement something, you give it for review. The reviewer shares their input, and you work on it. You send it again for review, and so on. Feedback is a continuous process wherein results are analysed, evaluated, and corrected until we get the desired one.

Exercise or Checkpoints:

	Question	Yes / No	Action if the answer is No and learning
1	Are you getting feedback on your work and working on continuous correction?		
2	Are you giving feedback on your peer work or colleagues to ensure continuous improvement?		
3	Are you applauding your team's or colleagues' or co-workers' work when they did distinguished work?		
4	Are you doing a self-review of your work?		

Summary

The current chapter highlights the importance of *continuous learning* in the software industry. It is essential for:

a. excelling in software career.

b. staying relevant to upcoming modern trends

Individuals must *adapt* to the rapid evolution of the following fast-growing items in the digital landscape:

- Tools

- Frameworks

- programming languages

- operating systems

- Processes and methodologies, and so on.

Individuals must include the following strategies for cultivating a continuous learning mindset:

- Setting SMART goals

- Creating dedicated schedules

- Cultivating curiosity

- Seeking regular feedback.

It introduces the Johari Window model to categorize areas of knowledge and emphasizes the importance of shared and individual growth in technical expertise.

Further, to enhance knowledge and the skillsets of professionals, the chapter explores diverse learning opportunities from the following areas viz:

- Online platforms: Udemy, Coursera and others.

- Technical conferences.

- Joining online communities.

- Seeking peer mentorship.

- Leveraging certifications.

- Open-source contributions.

Finally, the chapter focuses on the importance of feedback loops for propelling individual growth. Constructive feedback from mentors, co-workers and managers is essential for the following:

- Minimizes errors

- Accelerates learning.

Through consistent learning and feedback, professionals can:

- future-proof their careers,

- build confidence,

- earn respect.

This chapter inspires readers to embrace change and thrive in the river of knowledge.

Chapter 7

The Human Circuit: Powering Tech Teams with Emotional Intelligence

"Smooth seas do not make skilful sailors." This traditional proverb is a good way to understand emotional intelligence. Just as sailors become skilled by navigating rough waters, we develop emotional intelligence by facing challenges, managing stress, and understanding emotions—our own and those of others. Through these experiences, we grow stronger, improve our relationships, and become effective team players in the fast-paced world of software.

In a software company, you can't work alone; you will work within or lead teams. Emotional Intelligence plays a unique role here.

Emotional Intelligence is about managing emotions—both your own and those of others. Travis Bradberry, author of *Emotional Intelligence 2.0*, explains:

"Emotional Intelligence is all about:

a. Your potential to identify and understand emotions within yourself and others.

b. How you manage your behaviour and relationships using this awareness." (Bradberry & Greaves, 2009)

Figure 7.1: Emotional Intelligence

Emotional Intelligence(EI) is vital in professional life, especially in a team. Not everyone thinks the same, and conflicts are widespread when there is a difference in opinion. Every professional needs to understand their emotions and those of their fellow workers and act accordingly to create a healthy work atmosphere.

In the following sections, the chapter focuses on harnessing Emotional Intelligence in the software field.

Section 1: Importance of EI in the software industry
Section 2: Methods to cultivate self-awareness
Section 3: Implementing EI effectively.

Let's dive deep into these topics.

7.1 Why is emotional Intelligence crucial in software life?

Different vendors or different groups in the same organization collaborate to build products. It is the infrequent case that a single vendor or company owns every component of the product. In one way or another, they need to depend on other vendors or open source to build a working system. If you take a single organization, you can see various operating groups. It may be software development teams, QA, DevOps, IT, infrastructure teams, HR, facilities, innovation, etc. Even within groups, you do see a large number of professionals. As such, there could be chances of communication gaps, conflicts, adaptability issues or even stress with the environment or work. So, along with respective domain expertise, emotional Intelligence becomes equally important, which helps reduce conflicts, improve communications and creativity, and create a more cohesive working environment. Here we will discuss a little more details:

Conflicts Management in Software Life

Conflicts are common in software life, irrespective of groups, teams or even within teams. They can occur in respective domains, such as software architecture or implementation methodologies.

Figure 7.2: Conflicts Management

Sometimes, differences in opinions can lead to innovations. Still, at the same time, they can lead to non-functioning or even friction within the team, resulting in escalation to higher authorities. So, it is crucial to understand and calm down one's emotions and those of others. Emotional Intelligence plays a unique role(EI).

There can be tight deadlines sometimes when striving to market the business needs. So, almost every team may work under pressure (may be identical or on different occasions). Under such circumstances, individuals need to hold their nerves to calm down and help others accomplish business needs. For example:

Steve, a junior software developer at a software company, was working on a highly escalated customer defect that blocked a customer release. After he made code changes to address the defect, because of his inexperience, he received several code review comments from his senior fellow developers. Here, he respected review comments by addressing them meaningfully. Also, he realized that comments are for his personal development.

Exercise:

Have you come across any conflicts in your workplace? How did you resolve it?

	Conflicts	How it got resolved	If any key takeaway
1			
2			
3			
4			

Stress Management with Emotional Intelligence in the Software World

In modern days, stress management is one of the challenging aspects for most professionals, irrespective of age, gender, occupation, position held, etc. In some cases, the stress can reach extremes. Recently, I read in the newspaper that one of the software professionals died of a heart attack. I had seen a few more such instances earlier as well.

So, we need to find a way to overcome stress. Emotional Intelligence is one way to manage stress. People with higher EI will know stress factors and the tools or mechanisms to overcome them. These include reading and practising self-help books and effective time management.

Even though I wouldn't say I like stress, I have no option other than managing it. In my earlier experience, sometimes stress forced me to run away from things. Thanks to my mentor(s), manager(s) and senior colleague(s), who helped me overcome my stress phobia. Based on my journey, I've understood that constant stress doesn't just drain your focus—it takes a toll on your mind, body, and overall well-being. Also, we need to understand the difference between urgency and stress clearly. While the former is required to complete tasks, the latter will cause health issues. So decide what you need!

Even though you can't avoid 100% stress, you can manage it like diabetes. Some self-help books will guide you on how to prevent and manage stress. One of my favourite self-help books is *Ikigai: The Japanese Secret to a Long and Happy Life* by Francesc Miralles and Hector Garcia (*García & Miralles, 2016*). We should only consider the results after giving our 100% best effort. If something does not work your way, that's okay; try a different approach next time.

Nandini, a mid-level QA Analyst, worked at a software company and on a high revenue-generating project. Once, her senior colleague Fathima noticed Nandini was getting stressed out. She mentioned to Nandini that stress will take her nowhere and cause physical and mental health issues. Escalations are NOT meant to bring pressure but must be addressed with high priority by providing regular updates. If we give 100% effort, there will not be room for stress. Fathima also mentioned that escalations are manageable; it is about continuous work to find solutions and regularly update stakeholders. Here, Fathima exhibited emotional Intelligence.

Sometimes, we feel stressed because of the way we think. If your supervisor or customer asks for updates, instead of feeling stressed, give them details about your accomplishments with confidence and an optimistic note about what you will follow. Here, you will demonstrate emotional Intelligence in self.

Exercise:

Did you come across any stressful situations in your workplace? Fill details below:

	Stressful situation	How did you overcome it?	Is there any key takeaway for reusing the technique in the future?
1			
2			
3			
4			

Communication and Collaboration in the Software Industry

In scenarios where agile methodologies are applied, scrum meetings, product planning, hiring, training, event planning, etc., collaboration and communication play vital roles. They also play essential roles in business handling across multiple organizations, from product development to negotiations. So, emotional Intelligence plays a unique role in these cases.

As mentioned earlier, emotional intelligence enables professionals to manage stress effectively and build stronger communication and teamwork. It is essential for every software professional because it helps reduce stress and anxiety, encourages openness to honest feedback, and helps resolve conflicts within teams and with others outside the team. Emotional intelligence also boosts productivity and is key to developing healthy working relationships. Professionals are better equipped to grow and succeed in their careers with these skills. These skills are emphasized by Bradberry and Greaves (2009) in *Emotional Intelligence 2.0* as essential for managing stress, enhancing communication, resolving conflicts, and boosting productivity in professional settings.

A typical example is "retrospective meetings" conducted at the end of every sprint in the companies that adopted Agile methodologies(refer to Chapter 3). Here, individuals usually express their concerns or views on the ongoing methods, processes, practices, or anything blocking things concerning scrum work. Other team members share their opinions on the concerns and give their views on addressing them. In this meeting, people will take the opportunity to help each other to drive work more smoothly. They also take this occasion to express kudos to individuals for the exceptional work done by the team. Emotional Intelligence is unique in the work environment and impacts EI communication and collaboration.

7.2 Self-Awareness: Key to Team Dynamics

Awareness of your emotions is the starting point for developing emotional intelligence. Psychologist *Daniel Goleman* highlighted *self-awareness* as a foundational component of emotional intelligence in his ground breaking book *Emotional Intelligence* (1995). You must first understand what's happening inside you to practise emotional intelligence effectively. It means identifying emotional triggers when your mind reacts impulsively—which can cause issues for you and others around you. Without this self-awareness, you might unintentionally contribute to a toxic work environment.

Knowing your emotions, handling them appropriately, and practising self-regulation are crucial. Goleman explains that self-awareness improves emotional control, fostering healthier team dynamics. Without it, emotions can spiral, leading to unnecessary conflicts.

For example, suppose you're a software developer who made changes to a feature for a product in the software development team. You might feel insulted or demoralised if a peer unintentionally mocks your changes. As Travis Bradberry and Jean Greaves highlight in *Emotional Intelligence 2.0* (2009), your initial reaction is usually driven by emotional triggers. Still, by being aware of those triggers, you can shift your response consciously.

So, instead of reacting with anger or frustration, a more emotionally intelligent approach might be:

"I appreciate your feedback. Considering our sprint timelines, would you suggest a better approach that aligns with our current guidelines?"

This reframing—also supported by Douglas Stone et al. in *Difficult Conversations* (1999)—transforms what could be a defensive or tense moment into a collaborative one. They suggest that such phrasing acknowledges emotion while maintaining a tone of respect and open dialogue.

Things have changed in modern times, and many people have adopted emotional Intelligence. It is good practice to lean towards constructive feedback, as it is one of the continuous improvement sources. Now, let's dive into this to understand it better.

Tracing Emotional Aspects

In the software field, emotional triggers can occur for various reasons. They might be due to (not limited to) tight schedules or hard deadlines, unexpected issues that delay work, or complex problems that demand intense focus. Sometimes, unhealthy conversations, micromanagement, business loss, or job insecurity add emotional strain. Poor time management and the inability to cope with fast-paced growth can lead to frustration. Even something as routine as a code review can trigger emotions, especially if the feedback isn't delivered constructively.

As discussed, becoming aware of these triggers is the first step toward emotional clarity. This awareness helps us pause, reflect, and respond more effectively—in our personal development and team collaboration.

What Are Your Strengths And Areas of Improvements?

As discussed earlier, recognizing our strengths and areas for growth deepens self-awareness and improves how we interact in teams. If we know these, we can script our awareness and react accordingly. For example, an HR specialist might be trained in recruitment strategy, while a technical manager is powerful in technical aspects. Here, HR specialists can get help from technical managers for the hiring process, while a hiring manager can get support from an HR specialist for hiring-related processes and guidelines.

Similarly, on the software development side, you might be vital in protocol development, while your colleague can be an expert in user interface(UI) development. Both can collaborate on application development. Here, your colleague might need to improve protocol development, while you need to be familiar with UI development.

If individuals cannot access their abilities, they either ignore their capabilities(under commitment) or make unnecessary extra commitments. So, it is essential to recognize your strengths and areas for improvement to increase your self-awareness.

Exercise:

Identify your strengths and areas of improvement :

	Strengths	Area of improvements	Corrective actions
1			
2			
3			
4			

How Do You Handle Emotions in Groups and Teams

In software, teams generally consist of a specified number of individuals based on their expertise. Everyone will have a different mindset, and how everyone reacts to situations might differ. Frustrations, disappointments, impatience, and excitement are widespread like every human. As discussed earlier, when people understand their emotions well, they respond calmly and avoid overreacting, even under pressure. Being self-compassionate (as discussed earlier), they work towards growth. Such people try to maintain calmness in any situation by taking the necessary steps to manage their emotions.

Here is an example of handling emotions:

Manasa, a recruitment specialist in well-known organizations, had to visit a college for campus placement per her organization's needs. Initially, she felt nervous about giving presentations to 500-600 college students. Everyone was expecting a speech from her. She expected such things because she was self-aware. With her awareness and laser focus, she delivered a beautiful presentation.

Exercise:

Identify the emotional stress scenarios you have faced, and document thoughts of self-awareness and their impact or takeaways.

	Emotional stress	Self-awareness thoughts	Actions/Takeaways
1			
2			
3			
4			

Building Trust and Psychological Safety

Self-awareness is closely tied to building trust and fostering psychological safety. According to organisational psychologist *Amy C. Edmondson*, when professionals open up about their concerns, give frank feedback, and admit their mistakes, they foster psychological safety—a key ingredient for effective teamwork. Such vulnerability deepens interpersonal trust when supported by confidentiality and mutual respect.

Edmondson, A. C. (2019). *The Fearless Organization: Creating Psychological Safety in the Workplace for Learning, Innovation, and Growth*. Hoboken, NJ: Wiley.

Since they are free to express their opinions, teams can group and generate innovative ideas for official work (e.g., project discussions, client meetings), which benefits the organisation. Self-awareness can enhance effective communication, creative thinking, and problem-solving abilities when individuals feel psychologically safe. When we feel safer and psychologically unrestricted, we will concentrate on ideas and processes with an open mind. With that state, ideas will be flowing. Such collaborative meetings, commonly referred to as *brainstorming sessions*, are widely recognised as effective methods to generate innovative ideas. Here, professionals must remember to show "empathy" towards their colleagues. It makes them feel comfortable and allows them to open up. If the necessity arises, help them, which not only unblocks them but also assists in building trust in professional life. So, when you exhibit such traits, there will be no hesitation in their mind. During this process, there are no correct or incorrect thoughts or ideas, and members will welcome every thought or idea in the meeting before the final review to arrive at a relevant solution.

Exercise:

The following exercise questions are designed to help teams practically apply foundational concepts such as psychological safety (Edmondson, 2019) and emotional intelligence (Goleman, 1995) discussed in this chapter. These questions reflect widely accepted best practices in team collaboration, empathy, open communication, and continuous improvement. The exercises themselves are original content created to encourage self-reflection and actionable steps within professional teams.

	Areas	Self-Questions	Yes or No	Action Items in Case "No."
1	Create a Psychologically Safe Environment	Are you implementing a culture where team members feel safe while expressing their opinions without fear of judgment or criticism?		

2	Organize Brainstorming Sessions	Have you scheduled dedicated sessions for project discussions and idea generation?		
		Have you clearly defined the purpose and goals of the session to keep the focus aligned?		
		Are you encouraging all participants to contribute by establishing ground rules for respect and active listening?		
3	Practice and Promote Empathy	Have you actively listened to team members and recognized their contributions?		
		Offer support or assistance when someone faces challenges, showing that their well-being and input matter.		
4	Encourage Open-Mindedness	Have you communicated to participants that all ideas are valuable and that the goal is to generate a wide range of perspectives before arriving at a solution?		
		During brainstorming phase, are you avoiding labelling ideas as "right" or "wrong"?		
5	Build Trust Through Collaboration	Are you actively supporting colleagues who need help during discussions or tasks, reinforcing team collaboration?		

		Are you publicly recognizing and appreciating team member's contributions to strengthen trust and confidence?		
6	Develop Self-Awareness Among Team Members	Are you encouraging reflective practices like journaling or self-assessment to improve communication, creative thinking and problem-solving skills?		
		Are you providing resources or training sessions on emotional Intelligence and psychological safety?		
7	Facilitate Open Communication	Are you regularly checking with team members to understand their concerns or suggestions?		
		Are you providing anonymous feedback channels to ensure everyone has a voice, even if they feel shy speaking up in groups?		
8	Focus on Continuous Improvement	After brainstorming sessions, are you reviewing the process and outcomes with the team to identify improvements for future sessions?		
		Are you encouraging feedback on whether psychological safety and inclusiveness were adequately maintained in the team or group?		

7.3 Collaborations: Applying Emotional Intelligence Effectively

The emotional quotient is a parameter used to measure emotional Intelligence. In the software world, collaboration is the only thing that works. Whether across different business organizations, within organizations, across groups, across teams, or within teams, irrespective of any teams, they all work together to cater to business needs. The work environment is directly related to the quality of the emotional quotient(EQ). Conflicts are common while working across different business entities. Emotional Intelligence uniquely improves the overall productive activity of teams, groups and organizations and fosters mutual respect, creativity and professional relationships. *(Goleman, 1995).*

In the following section, let's discuss applying emotional Intelligence in a collaborative environment.

Resolving Conflicts in IT World

Conflicts are inevitable while working in a team(s). Like in real life, there are no specific reasons for such disputes in the software world; they can occur for various reasons. However, one can handle the conflicts. Usually, a leader manager or someone in a higher position can handle disputes. Here, emotional Intelligence plays a unique role. People with emotional Intelligence can resolve disputes by respecting individual opinions, discussing the pros and consequences of each approach, practice, tool, or methodology for the organization's benefit, and creating good work ethics and a healthy work atmosphere.

For example, if we are a software development team, conflicts arise if there are differences in opinions concerning architectural approach, development methods, tools, framework that individuals use, code reviews, etc. Conflicts need not be in the form of heated arguments, but they can arise due to differences in thoughts. Here, the primary aim is to identify the source of conflict and foster better understanding. Effective conflict resolution requires empathy, patience, and the ability to manage emotions. Some techniques like compromise, collaboration and negotiation are often applied to work towards solutions. More focus should be on the issues rather than individuals and work towards the benefit of everyone.

Jayanth and Jyotsna are two software developers working in a software company with Avantika, their software development manager. Both developed different parts of the business product. Regarding automation, Jayanth wanted to use the existing legacy framework for its simplicity, while Jyotsna wished to use the new ROBOT framework (https:// robotframework.org) for its portability. They must find a way to overcome these conflicts and work toward development completion. After carefully listening to both individuals, she asked to do a proof of concept(POC) as a neutral solution within the stipulated timeline. So, with her emotional Intelligence, Avantika helped the team resolve the conflicts without interrupting business needs.

Exercise:

Identify if any conflicts arise in your work environment and journal in the table below on how you resolved them.

	Conflicts	How you resolved	Key takeaways
1			
2			
3			
4			

a) Communication and Emotional Intelligence in Software World

Have you ever wondered why communication is so crucial in your professional life? It is vital as it builds a virtual channel for exchanging ideas, thoughts, opinions, negotiations, and feedback within and outside organizations. It can range from as simple as between two people to as complex as among multiple organizations. So, communication plays a significant role in the software world.

When you present your ideas or workflow to people across different geographical regions, you must exhibit emotional Intelligence. It means you must adjust your presentation skills by explaining things so everyone can understand what you are presenting. Here, communication plays a unique role. Emotional Intelligence helps to achieve that to some extent.

Greeshma is a product owner in a well-known organization. Here is a clear illustration of how her emotional Intelligence helped her to cater for the business needs:

She works in a group geographically distributed across India, Japan, Australia, and the USA. She is presenting a roadmap for the product for the next two years. She needs to adjust her communication skills during her presentation so everyone can understand, even though their assents vary. Here, she sticks to the basics of communication, which is clear, concise and controlled. Her emotional Intelligence gives her a chance to improve her communication further.

Developing Empathy

Empathy involves recognizing and understanding the feelings or emotions of others - is a foundational skill in emotional intelligence, *as emphasized by Daniel Goleman* in *Emotional Intelligence.* It leads to greater compassion and support. It is one of the critical qualities required for communication and leadership. Empathy nurtures human relationships and helps convey ideas in better way. Leaders and team members who show empathy can resolve/avoid conflicts at work. It will help win the confidence of people on the other side(it may be a leader or team member) and make them feel valued.

Henry, a data science engineer in a software company, used to work in the office longer. His manager observed the stress and anxiety that Henry was facing and approached him for discussion.

The manager said, *"It seems you are stressed out. You might need a break. Let's discuss and replan your work to make it stress-free after your time off."*

It shows how the manager empathizes with Henry and makes him feel good. It also encourages a healthy atmosphere and is open to honest communication.

b) Collaborative Culture:

Emotional Intelligence contributes to a collaborative culture wherein individuals feel supported, motivated and valued.

Action Items:

	Areas	Self-Questions	Yes or No	Action Items in Case "No."
1	Prioritize Clear Communication	Are you emphasizing communicating ideas in a precise, considerate and controlled manner?		
		Are you tailoring your presentation style to suit the audience's cultural and linguistic background?		
		Are you adjusting your tone, language and examples to ensure your message is conveyed to the team?		
		Are you staying calm and composed, especially during high-stakes discussions or disagreements?		
		After presentations or discussions, ask for feedback to improve your communication skills further.		

2	Active listening	Are you listening to understand what others say without interrupting?		
		Are you able to understand the speaker's emotions accurately?		
3	Empathy Journal	At the end of every day, are you journaling your situation and how you interacted with everyone?		
		Question yourself whether you understand their feelings.		
		Ask yourself how you can be more empathetic.		
4	Empathy mapping	As a reflective action, think about some person and ask below questions: 1. What do they say? 2. What do they do? 3. What do they think? 4. What do they feel?		

By answering and cultivating these, you will be able empathy for your colleagues or co-workers.

Summary

Emotional Intelligence(EI) is mandatory in a collaborative environment, especially in IT. It involves understanding the emotions of a) oneself and b) others and behaving accordingly. It is essential for fostering a healthy working environment and improving work culture.

Why is emotional intelligence (EI) important?

Collaboration across vendors and teams is expected in a software company, but sometimes, it can lead to potential communication gaps, conflicts, and stress. EI helps reduce conflicts, improve communication, foster creativity, and build cohesive teams.

- **Conflict Management Handling:** Conflicts often arise in areas like software architecture or implementation methods. EI helps professionals manage emotions, address conflicts constructively, and leverage differences for innovation. Example: Junior developers learn and grow from constructive feedback.

- **Practising Stress Management:** Stress is prevalent in high-pressure software environments. EI equips professionals to manage stress through self-awareness, prioritization, and continuous learning. Example: Effective mentoring helps professionals handle escalations calmly.

- **Fostering Communication and Collaboration:** EI enhances communication in agile practices like scrum and retrospectives. Professionals with high EI foster open dialogue, resolve concerns, and celebrate achievements. EI is critical for building strong professional relationships and boosting productivity.

Cultivating Self-Awareness for Team Dynamics:

- **Self-Awareness**: Understand and manage emotions to prevent toxic environments.

- **Handling Triggers**: Manage stress from deadlines and feedback constructively.

- **Strengths & Weaknesses**: Identify personal skills and gaps for better collaboration.

- **Team Emotions**: Stay calm and encourage growth during challenges.

- **Trust & Safety**: Foster open communication, empathy, and team creativity.

- **Exercises**: Reflect on stress, promote safe spaces, and encourage emotional intelligence training.

Collaborations: Applying Emotional Intelligence Effectively

- Emotional Intelligence (EQ) enhances collaboration by fostering mutual respect, creativity, and effective conflict resolution.

- Differing opinions can cause conflict in teams, but EQ helps leaders resolve disputes by promoting understanding, patience, and solution-focused communication.

- Effective communication, aided by EQ, tailors presentations to diverse audiences, ensuring clarity and adaptability.

- Empathy improves relationships and helps resolve conflicts by understanding others' emotions fostering trust and support.

- A collaborative culture is built through EQ, motivating and valuing individuals.

- Action items to strengthen team dynamics include prioritizing clear communication, active listening, empathy journaling, and empathy mapping.

Chapter 8

Visionary Coding: Crafting Your Career Path

"Your career is your responsibility. Your ability to set goals, plan, and execute is the most important factor in your success."

– Brian Tracy

Note: This quote is commonly attributed to Brian Tracy. For similar concepts, refer to Tracy, B. (2004). Goals! Berrett-Koehler.

Visionary coding in the software field refers to innovative, forward-thinking or vision. It is like how you are coding as per your vision. It highlights creative ways to solve problems, methodologies, routes to leverage modern trends to build innovative solutions, and the long-term vision of organisations, groups and individuals. For every individual, a well-defined vision is required to excel in the software field irrespective of whether software developer, QA, architect, project manager, director, VP, all-level HRs, marketing and even CEOs, entrepreneurs, etc. So, your future in the software field depends on how you craft your career path.

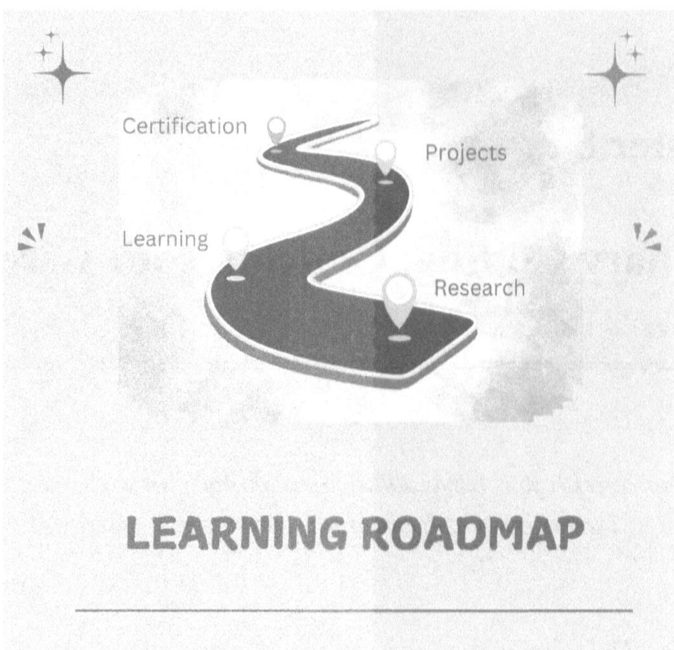

Figure 9.1: A sample learning roadmap

In this chapter, we will learn how to harness the power of visualisation, explore strategies for crafting a career path, and ultimately, how to align career goals with personal values in the software world. Here, I will use the example of a *software developer*, but individuals can apply the idea presented here to most roles in the software profession and personal life as well.

Note: The visualization techniques such as creating mental pictures, focusing on the process, including emotional elements, and building a vision board are inspired by Shakti Gawain's work in Creative Visualization *(Gawain, 2020).*

8.1 The Power of Visualization: Imagining Your Success

Visualisation is a powerful technique that encourages us to work towards our future (in this context, career) vision. It involves creating a picture in your mind that depicts the accomplishments you want to achieve as *already* done. It allows us to experience success and motivates us to work towards our vision.

When you define your career vision, you must practice it. So, before that, you need a motivational force to drive you towards the endpoint. *Visualization* helps to achieve this. If you imagine success has already happened, it will excite you, which motivates and energizes your mind and helps build laser focus.

Note: This idea is beautifully explained in Rhonda Byrne's *The Secret*, which focuses on the Law of Attraction—the belief that focusing on positive outcomes can attract those outcomes into our lives. Similarly, as mentioned earlier, Shakti Gawain's *Creative Visualization* describes how imagining success can reprogram our subconscious mind, align our energies, and open doors to the possibilities we seek (Byrne, 2006; Gawain, 2020).

Visualization Benefits

a. **Uphill your motivation** – As mentioned above, Visualization helps motivate you to work toward your vision.

b. **Laser Focus** – Your focus will get improved.

c. **Improved problem-solving** fosters creativity and helps increase your problem-solving ability.

8.2 Defining Your Career Vision as a Software Developer

Chapter 6 discussed time management, goal setting, to-do lists, etc. However, those goals are short-term, like learning one more programming language, databases, frameworks, operating systems, best practices, and soft skills like strategic and critical thinking.

However, career vision refers to a broader realm wherein you will set long-term goals, maybe skills you want to develop over time, positions you want to pursue, and the business you want to do professionally and personally. You will be aligned with what you need to accomplish over time. For that, you need to be resilient to challenges or setbacks in your personal or professional life and adopt a growth mindset to reach your vision.

a. Key components

Here are the critical components of career vision.

a. **Long-term goals**: This is the primary step in career vision, wherein goals need to be very clear, whether for a position, entrepreneurship, or pursuing a master's or PhD or anything. It purely depends on the individuals. If you are a software developer, your vision can be to be a principal developer, software architect, BU head, project manager, director, VP, or CEO. Again, it purely depends on individual interests. To pursue such roles, you must acquire the necessary skill set to pursue the position. So, your long-term goals need to concentrate on acquiring corresponding skills and ensure you have a daily day for that.

As an exercise, define a long-term career goal.

	Current role or position	**Long term goals**
1	Software Developer	Software Architect or Development Manager
2		
3		
4		

b. **Professional Aspirations**: Unlike acquiring a position, professional aspiration is all about what you want to achieve over a long time in software life. It can be knowledge and experience of cutting-edge technologies, becoming a professional or career coach, building a product to address critical problems or make things easier, building a start-up, increasing job opportunities, etc.

Fill in the table below:

	Current State	**Long term Aspiration**
1	Nothing, only theoretical knowledge	Building a product
2		
3		
4		

c. **Personal Satisfaction**: Career vision is not limited to accomplishment but is also related to personal fulfilment. Your career vision should also provide satisfaction and make your accomplishment more valuable and meaningful. Some people often ask, "*Are you happy with what you are doing in your job?*" That happiness should be part of your career vision.

Fill in the table below on personal satisfaction.

	Questions	**Have satisfaction (Yes/No)**
1	Are you happy with the company you are working with?	
2	Are you happy with the project you are working with?	
3	Are you happy with the technology you are working with?	
4	Are you learning from the project you are working with?	
5	Are you happy with the work environment?	
6	Are you happy with your compensation?	
7	Are you happy with your peers and colleagues?	
8	Are you able to grow up on the ladder?	
9	Are you getting time to do personal work as well?	

If you answered yes to all the questions above, you are blessed with a beautiful work environment. Say thanks to God from the bottom of your heart.

b. Steps to define your career vision

Here are some valuable steps you need to follow to achieve your career vision.

Reflect on your passion: Progress is impossible without action. You are responsible for nurturing your passion and discovering what excites you about your work. As a software developer, is it crafting intricate logic for a specific feature, tackling challenging problems, building solutions from scratch, exploring DevOps methodologies, or staying ahead with continuous learning in cutting-edge technologies? The possibilities are endless.

Exercise:

Fill in the below table:

	Identify Your Passion	Mention Why it Makes You Happy?	How is it helpful to you or your career?
1			
2			
3			
4			
5			

Identifying these factors will help you add deeper meaning to your accomplishments and drive you toward greater success.

Vision about the ideal future: Visualise your perfect future and fill in the table below:

Exercise:

Fill the table below as per your career vision:

	Question on Career Vision	After One Year	After 5 Years	After 10 Years
1	Where will you be working?			
2	On what technologies are you working?			
3	What is your position?			
4	Did you own a company?			
5	Imagine the type of people you are dealing with which adds value to you and your career.			

Similarly, you can have a vision for relationship, well-being, money(or wealth), and spirituality.

Create a visualisation map, which some people call a vision board for your career and personal goals, if any. Here are sample vision board areas:

Figure 9.2: A Sample Vision Board on HRMRSC

Align with your strengths: Your career vision must align with your strengths. For example, if you are an HR trainee, you can set a long-term career vision as becoming Chief Human Resource Officer. If you are a software developer, you can have wide-open options: You can become chief technology officer(CTO), vice president of engineering(VP), software architect, or a distinguished engineer, or you can even start your own company. As part of the vision, identify your core strength area and consider developing soft skills., ex: critical thinking, strategic planning, empathy, emotional intelligence, communication and teamwork) and how you can use them to reach your vision.

Exercise:

	Current Position	Career Vision	Skills Required to achieve the same
1			
2			
3			

Incorporating values and Lifestyle: Your career vision is not just about accomplishment, which you had set as a long-term vision. It also needs to add value to your achievements and your lifestyle. Make sure to put a career vision that makes you burn out regularly, but set your vision so that you can still find work-life balance. Flexibility here and there might not disturb your career vision.

Building a routine to accomplish your career vision would help. To create your routines, refer to *Chapter 14: The Ritual Algorithm: Programming Success into Your Life*.

c. Benefits of Career Vision

Improve your decision-making capability: Improve your decision-making capability: When the technology selection is clear, you can select the right path since you already have a clear vision.

Motivation: Whenever you solve complex problems, you will not get frustrated; instead, you will get motivated, as you think the problem you are solving right now aligns with your career vision. Imagine you are running a company, and a similar situation occurs, so how do you resolve it at that time? It will help you get motivated and perform much better.

Consistency in Growth: I have seen a few people say, I work only for money, no matter what. What will happen to career vision in the software field in such cases? Such people will need a clearer vision, and you can't expect Growth. On the other hand, if you have a clear-cut career vision, with every action you take, you know what you are doing and work more towards meeting your career goal. Here, as mentioned earlier chapters, *Dweck's* concept of a *growth mindset* helps you reach your career vision.

d. Visualization Exercise

We have reached one of the most essential highlights of the chapter, i.e. **practising Visualization**. Here are a few techniques we can do the same:

a. **Create Mental Picture**: Close your eyes, after a few breaths (in Sanskrit, it is called Pranayama, although it has a broader definition), start imaging your future, which is close to your vision; include specific details:

1	Where are you working?
2	With whom are you working?
3	With whom are you collaborating regularly?
4	In what project are you working?

b. **Please focus on the process rather than the result**: Of course, it is essential to visualize the end goal, but it is equally important to visualize the journey towards the end goal, which could consist of challenges you have faced, overcoming procrastination, setbacks, resilience towards hindrances, etc. By creating such Visualization with mental pictures, you will not be surprised when you face such things in real life and will take action to overcome them..

c. **Emotional Elements:** Visualizing your accomplishment will excite, fulfil, or even make you grateful. It will enhance your motivation and help you focus your efforts. .

d. **Regular Practice**: Practice Visualization every day, probably before bed and soon after waking up. You can write down a script for visualization, record it with your voice, and listen to it daily. Some motivational music and with your voice will beautify things and make them more effective.

e. **Vision Board**: This is another powerful visualization technique. It can be physical or digital. It should consist of your long-term vision. Seeing this every day will help you align with your long-term aspirations.

Note: I am not an expert in visualisation or breathing exercise. For this activity, you can contact experts in that area of your choice or refer YouTube videos from experts. I learnt from workshop of my mentor Dr. Manjunath, a mind performance coach and the author of the book "Unleashing The Power of Reading". The breathing exercise called Pranayama has roots in ancient yogic traditions (Iyengar, 1993).

8.3 Aligning Career Goals with Personal Values in Tech

Long-term goal accomplishment is an essential factor in achieving career vision. But it is not the only factor. Adding personal value to your career vision is equally vital. You need to ensure it will add value to your overall work. Values refer to a sense of accomplishment, satisfaction, and confidence in doing further things.

a. Why Values Matter?

- **Source of fulfilment** - Once you reach your career aspiration according to your vision, you will experience a sense of satisfaction.

- **Beliefs** - that guide your decisions and actions. They also help you realize the true meaning of success.

- **Realize** - a deep sense of purpose.

b. How do you identify your values?

You can identify your values in the following ways.

a. How did you feel when you fixed your first bug(if you are a developer)? How did you feel when you found a critical bug in the software(if you are from QA), or how did you feel when you found the right candidate when you were part of the hiring team? Or how did you feel when you got your first patent?

   Reflecting on your experience will help you to identify your values.

b. Have you ever thought about the core values that resonate with you? Can you list them out? I will help you here with some of them:

   1. Creativity

   2. Innovation

   3. Work-life balance

   4. Collaboration

   5. Problem-solving

   6. Creating a positive impact on your surroundings

   There could be many more; please list them to identify your values.

   As an exercise, kindly fill in your core values in the table below.

	Your Core Values
1	
2	
3	
4	

The list can be huge, but what matters is: what matters to you most?

It will help your decision-making skills.

c. How can you align your values with career goals?

Let's explore the connection between aligning values and career goals.

Evaluating Career Goals: Our career goals must align with our core values; otherwise, adjustments are needed. For instance, if you deeply value a healthy work-life balance but struggle to attain it in your current role, then it might be worth exploring a new project opportunity. You don't always need to switch jobs, but you can identify the right project within your organisation that aligns with your goals. Consider another case wherein you value innovation in your work; however, your job lacks creativity. Here, you need to rethink changing professional direction. Justify yourself if you are on the right path to achieving your vision. This alignment is crucial for personal satisfaction and avoiding conflicts.

Decisions based on values: Whenever you encounter career-based choices, ensure they align with your values. Accept opportunities that align with your vision, regardless of the position or monetary compensation.

Trade-offs: Sometimes, it is challenging for anyone to make choices between opportunities and values. It is often tempting to accept a high-paying job offer, even if it does not align with our values. However, we should consider the long-term benefits. If the offer is high-paying and aligns with your career goals, then you're lucky; embrace it. If the job offer has an average pay yet aligns with your career vision, we can consider it as well. If a job pays a high salary but not with your values, think it over again before you accept. If the pay is average and not aligned with your career goals, it's best not to take it. However, there are several aspects to consider, such as whether you are looking for a job after a layoff or an extended career break, in which case you should make a decision based on what matters most at that time. But if you are well settled in your job and your financial position is good, then make choices as mentioned above.

Exercise:

	Career goal Self Evaluation	Yes or No	Action Item to align your goal
1	Is your professional life aligned with your career goal?		

Benefits of Aligning Career Goals with Values:

The advantages of aligning to career goals are Authenticity, long-term motivations and dependency fulfilment.

Summary

Visionary Coding: Encourages forward-thinking and innovative solutions in software careers, applicable to all roles from developers to CEOs.

Power of Visualization:

- Engages the brain, boosts confidence, and strengthens emotional commitment.

- Practice daily, focusing on the journey and end goals.

Benefits: Improved decision-making, motivation, and consistent growth through a clear vision.

Defining Career Vision:

- Set long-term goals for desired roles or aspirations.

- Align vision with professional and personal satisfaction, leveraging strengths and passions.

Steps to Career Vision: Reflect on passions, visualize your ideal future, align goals with strengths, and maintain work-life balance.

Chapter 9

Planting Seeds of Innovation: Cultivating Creativity and Problem-Solving Skills for Growth

"Necessity is the mother of invention"

– Ancient proverb, often attributed to Plato

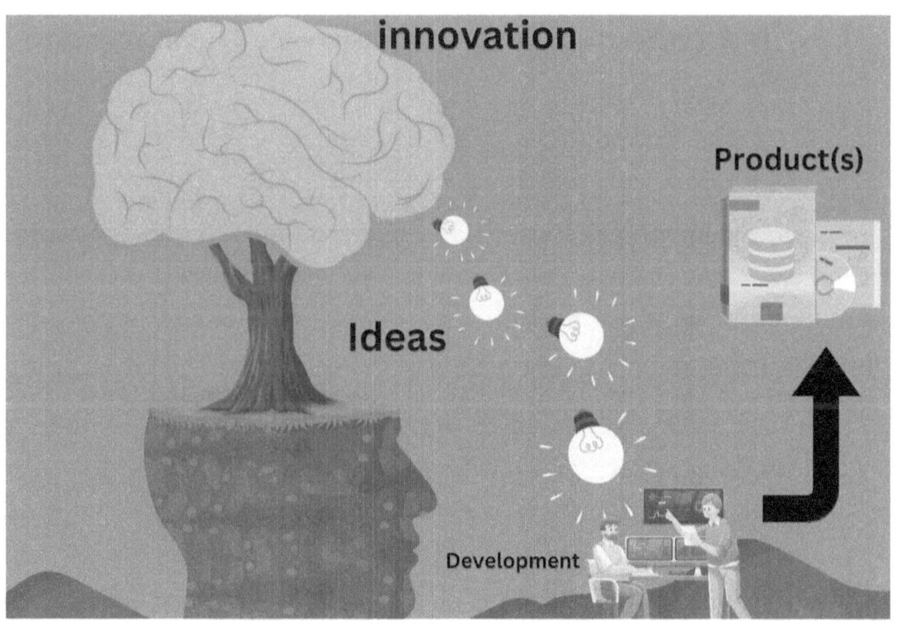

Figure 10.1: Sample mechanism of Turning Ideas into Products

When we have a strong desire to solve a problem, our mind naturally begins to search for different ways to fix it. With steady effort and the tools we have, we eventually find a solution. For example, in the past, washing clothes by hand was a laborious task. This challenge led to the invention of the washing machine. Similarly, the need to communicate while on the move led to the development of mobile phones and wireless technology. These are excellent examples of how challenges give rise to creative ideas. It all depends on how we think. If we bring this same mindset into our profession—while building new features, fixing bugs, automating tasks, or leading teams—creativity and problem-solving make a big difference. These skills became the primary criteria for distinguishing any software professional. It is the responsibility of the professional to develop and enhance such skills. This chapter will discuss practical techniques to improve "*Creative Thinking*" and "*Problem-Solving mindset*" and share a few real-world examples of innovative solutions in the software world.

9.1 Why Creativity Matters in Software Development?

Creativity is about developing new ideas and finding a unique and effective solution to problems. The better creative technique you use, the better the solution will become. Creativity plays a unique role while developing new architecture, designs, feature developments, bug fixing, automation framework, dev ops methodologies, and agile methodologies, even during recruitment, employment management, company business investments, and other relevant ones.

Fathima, a software developer in a prestigious company, is working on a networking project. Her feature requires one to look up a particular record ID amongst the list of records. There were millions of such records. Her initial approach was linear search, which could have been proficient as it took longer to search if the record ID was present at the end. She has to use her creative mindset to arrive at a better solution. Being an intelligent developer, Fathima realized that someone had already stored records in sorted order, so she used the binary search method to find the record, which proved to be one of the best solutions and improved her feature solution. So, Fathima could solve real-world problems with her creative mindset.

Creative Thinking is not limited to software development; it plays a unique role in different areas of the software industry. For example, applying creativity in Agile will help manage projects and sprints effectively. If a SCRUM master is creative, they can utilize project resources effectively.

Joseph works as a Scrum Master at a software company. One of his key responsibilities is assigning Scrum stories to team members for each sprint. Each team member is typically allocated work equivalent to an 8-point story. However, at the end of a particular sprint planning session, Joseph was left with a single 5-point story after assigning sufficient work to the rest of the team. Assigning this 5-point story would have resulted in an imbalance, leaving the team underutilized for that sprint.

To solve the problem, Joseph had to think creatively and come up with a practical solution. After considering his options, he realized that swapping stories between sprints could work, as long as it stayed within the current Program Increment. With this in mind, he replaced the 5-point story in the current sprint with an 8-point story from the next sprint and assigned it to a team member. This smart adjustment allowed him to balance the team's workload effectively, ensuring they remained productive while staying aligned with the sprint's goals.

9.2 Techniques for Enhancing Creative Thinking

This section will examine how effectively we can increase creative Thinking in the software industry.

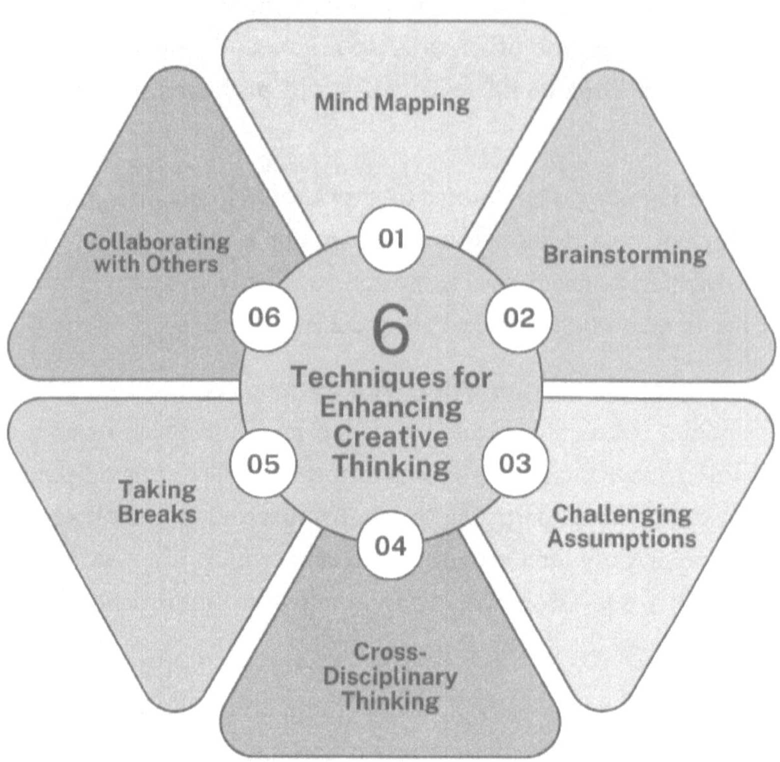

Figure: 10.2: Strategies to Improve Creative Thinking

These techniques will not come naturally, but one can develop with continuous practice.

Mind Mapping as mentioned in Chapter 2, is a visualization technique that starts with a central idea and branches into possible subproblems relevant to that idea. It helps break more significant problems into smaller and easily manageable ones. Individuals can work on sub-problems by keeping a designated time frame.

Here is the sample mind map.

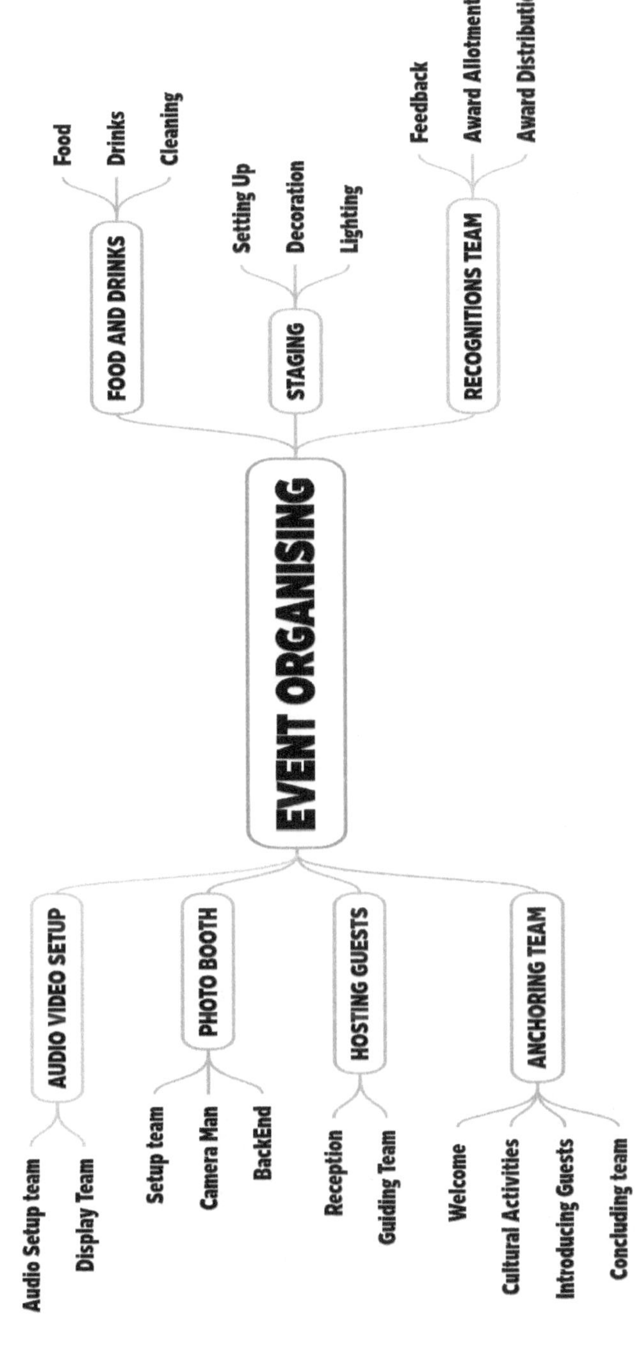

Figure 9.3 A sample Mindmap for Event Organisation

(Note: Above Mind map is created using Boardmix.)

Reshma, an HR manager in a software company, was given the responsibility for conducting the company's annual day event. The challenge started with distributing work among different HR and facility team members. Being a creative thinker, Reshma used the concept of Mind Map to break event tasks into smaller sub-tasks like staging, photo booth, audio video setup, reception, hosting guests, anchoring, distributing recognitions, food and drinks and assigning them to different groups and those groups into individual members. With this arrangement, they could distribute the work effectively for a successful event. Here, Reshma used her creative mindset to conduct an annual day event and finished in style.

Exercise:

Create a mindmap for your personal or professional project or your designs and journal for future reference.

Brainstorming: In this technique, people generate various ideas to solve problems in a quick session. There is no concept of good or bad ideas, and people don't care about it. The main intention is to generate new ideas to move towards problem resolution. Brainstorming can be done by a single person or in a group, but a group usually does it.

Figure 9.4: Brain Storming Sessions for Product Improvement

Organizations often tailor brainstorming to suit their unique culture. In some teams, brainstorming sessions are triggered during high-pressure situations—whether to solve critical issues or foster innovation. Once the problem is clearly understood, everyone in the team are need to (or can) express their thoughts or ideas freely without judgment. The goal is quantity over perfection. After the session, ideas are reviewed, sometimes combined, and tested through quick experiments to validate potential solutions.

Mentioning about usage of this technique in organisation is just an example. We can also apply this technique in our personal growth as well. Whether we think about new designs, solutions to complex problems or even for best practices, this technique is useful.

The brainstorming technique, popularized by advertising executive Alex F. Osborn in the 1940s, remains a powerful tool for generating creative ideas. For those interested in exploring it further, his seminal book *"Applied Imagination"* offers valuable insights.

Exercise:

Have you come across any brainstorming sessions in your project? If so, kindly do below exercise:

	Major Brain storming Idea	Have you participated actively?	What are your contribution?	How close is your idea to clearcut design or solution(%)?	Key take aways
1					

Challenging Assumptions: In most cases, there is always more than one approach to solving a problem. One way to boost our creativity is to challenge our assumptions. It stimulates our brain to think about alternative solutions, and if we can come up with alternative solutions, we can compare them and apply the best one to solve our problem. However, note down ideas as they might help solve future problems. Keeping open-minded when working on solutions is another crucial factor contributing to creative thinking.

Exercise:

	Did you come across multiple solution to same problems(Y/N)? If yes, list down the solution	Based on what criteria you arrived best solution?	Can your idea be reused in different scenarios?	What are your learnings?
1				
2				

Cross-Disciplinary Thinking: Ideas don't always have to come from code or software architectures. You can also gain powerful insights from everyday life. Just take a moment to observe your kitchen—the way your mom, wife, or both plan meals, reuse leftovers smartly, and make every ingredient count. Isn't that resource management at its best?

If we stay curious and keep our minds open, we'll start seeing patterns, techniques, and inspirations from other fields—and they can often give us breakthrough ideas for our work in tech. It's all about thinking beyond boundaries and applying those lessons creatively in the software world.

Exercise:

Identify the top five ideas you got from your personal life and applied in your software life.

	Ideas from other field
1	
2	
3	
4	
5	

Taking Breaks: Taking breaks is one of the most important things to do to avoid over exhaustion from work. It energizes your brain and helps prepare you for the next task. During working hours, most of us take coffee breaks, lunch breaks, tea breaks, and probably snack breaks as well. Frequent breaks are necessary to improve our thinking.

I have seen some people do their work even during breaks, but I recommend doing that only sometimes. If we prevent out brain from resting, our productivity might go down. Of course, we have no choices during crises, but we need not make it a regular habit.

Exercise:

	Questionnaire	Yes or No	If No, action item
1	Are you taking sufficient breaks without hampering work?		
2	Are you using the *pomodoro* technique for your learning or work?		
3	Are you discussing your project or work during break?		I don't recommend to talk about work during break.

On the other hand, sometime back I came across an article about a software company that encourages employees to sleep during lunch breaks (after lunch), which is a better strategy for energized minds. Some people, including myself, prefer to walk, as we get a better chance to expose ourselves to sunlight and improve our blood circulation. There could be different strategies as well. You can choose one that works for you.

Collaborating with Others:

In the software field, collaboration is essential—you can't work in isolation and expect to accomplish tasks effectively. Sharing your approaches and ideas with team members fosters a healthy exchange of knowledge and allows you to tap into the diverse ways people visualize and think. Everyone brings unique perspectives to the table. Sometimes, ideas from your colleagues are better than your ideas. Adopting them will elevate the quality of your work. Often, the best solutions emerge from a blend of your ideas and those of your peers. It stimulates creativity and opens the door to innovative solutions you might not have considered alone.

9.3 Encouraging a Problem-Solving Mindset

A creative mindset is undoubtedly essential, but *problem-solving* is equally important to accomplish your daily routines in your work. In the tech industry, problem-solving ranges from minor user interface bugs to production outages in case if you are a developer. It is not only confined to software architecture and development activities but also in the areas of automation, integrations, development operations(DevOps), testing, software releases, security, system upgrades, operating system and relevant software, hardware maintenance, physical servers, people management, human resource, facilities and others.

So, you need to have specific strategies to develop a problem-solving mindset. Here are some of them:

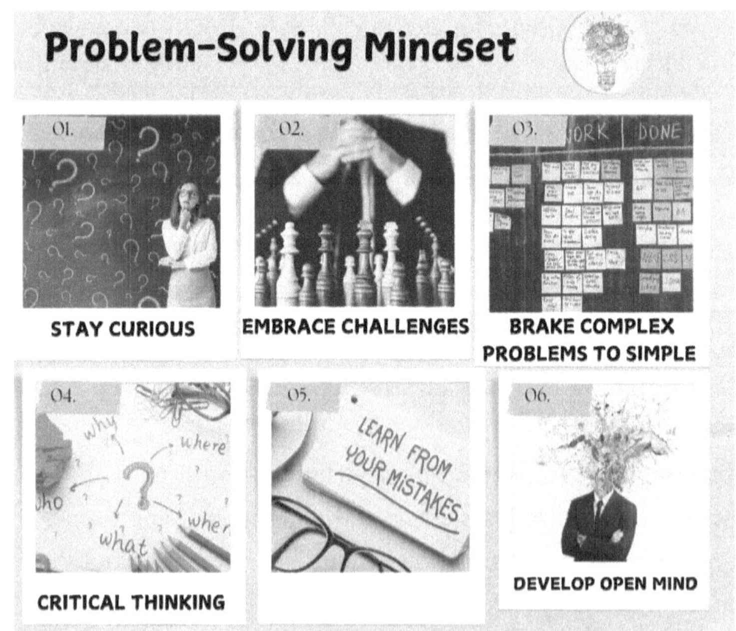

Figure 10.5: Problem Solving Techniques

Stay Curious:

It is essential to be curious about your work. Always observe things; if anything changes, find the root cause for the change confined within your work scope. It may be any change in software requirement, product behavioural change, change in software baseline, scripts, testing strategy and others.

Knowing "Why" will help you take any further action on "How" if required. For example, if you notice a change in a requirement document, you will likely realize any change in customer requirements. Make changes in your design, code, test, deployment, and other relevant areas.

	Questionnaire	Yes or No	If no, corrective Action
1	Are you curious about your work or project and technologies		

Embrace Challenges:

In your regular work, the problems you face and the solutions you discover are your stepping stones to growth. Some challenges can be frustrating, especially when they take days or weeks to solve. During these times, patience is your greatest ally. Persevere, work steadily toward a solution, and know that each hurdle adds to your invaluable experience.

Patience is not just a virtue but a critical factor in embracing and overcoming challenges.

Note: The following is a generalized scenario inspired by real-world software development challenges. It is intended to illustrate for educational purpose and does not refer to any specific company or proprietary project.

Rajeev, a software developer worked on a memory leak issue – a complex problem in a distributed system with minimum information. It took few months for him to diagnose and resolve issue. Imagine the patience, perseverance, and effort he demonstrated throughout that journey! His unwavering self-belief kept him motivated, maintaining hope and focus every step of the way.

He tackled the problem with scientific precision: forming hypotheses, running experiments, and meticulously documenting each challenge and approach. This documentation prevented repeated mistakes and served as a guide to keep him moving in the right direction. His story is a testament to the power of resilience, structured thinking, and the belief that no problem is insurmountable with the right mindset.

"You can embrace your challenges with your attitude and perseverance effort!".

Break Problems Down:

As discussed in previous chapters, individuals should break complex problems into smaller, manageable sub-problems and focus on solving one problem at a time. In my experience, it helps reduce stress and feelings of overwhelm while enhancing focus and clarity.

Critical Thinking

Critical thinking involves understanding and analysing problems, examining all available information, asking the right questions to fill in any gaps, and making decisions based on logic and data. Taking a methodical approach significantly increases the chances of arriving at the right solution. In software development, critical thinking is a vital skill that enables the evaluation of different solutions and the selection of the most effective one.

Note: The following is a generalized scenario inspired by real-world software QA challenges. It is intended to illustrate for educational purpose and does not refer to any specific company or proprietary project.

Svecha is a principal QA analyst at a software company working on a networking project. Her primary responsibility is to help the development team by simulating customer issues occurred in the field. However, because of the complexity of the problem, it was impractical to simulate the exact problem in the lab. Here, her responsibility is to mimic the environment around the problem. So, the problem needs a series of hypotheses. Svecha approached this with her "*Critical Thinking*", which required thorough understanding and narrowing down scenarios.

She started analysing the problem to find out:

1	What is happening?
2	Where it is happening?
3	How frequently the problem is happening?
4	What are the impacted modules ?
5	Whether the configuration that the customer is using is aligned with their expectation ?
6	Whether inputs are within the product specification limits ?
7	Is the problem is specific to particular parameters in the config ?
8	What is the behaviour if she changes the specific essential configuration ?
9	What is the end user impact ?
10	Is this revenue impacting problem ?

and other relevant areas.

After the initial analysis, she referred to the input information provided by the customer. With that, she determined:

1	The system input during problem occurrence is
2	The environment conditions like how many sessions
3	Type of the sessions
4	The maximum surge in traffic
5	Input patterns
6	Current system memory
7	Current resource usage
8	Any critical information like alarms
9	Product specific logs
10	Pattern repetition

11	System object usage details
12	Frequency of problem occurred in customer provinces
13	All threads running and healthy during scenarios

Also, Svecha asked the customer further questions to get maximum information. Once she felt she had sufficient information and, based on available logs, she could successfully simulate a miniature version of the problem in her lab.

So here, Svecha's *Critical Thinking* helped her perform her tasks promptly.

Similarly, critical Thinking can be applied to any area of the software profession, irrespective of position and experience.

Exercise:

Have you used critical thinking in your work? If so, fill below details:

	Scenario	Did you apply critical thinking: Yes or No?	Explain how your critical thinking helped to address the scenario?	Can you reuse this thinking in different scenario?
1				
2				
3				
4				

Learn from Mistakes:

Mistakes are an inevitable part of work life. The majority of our learning will happen through our own mistakes and teammates' mistakes. What truly matters is what we learn from them and ensure they aren't repeated. A proactive approach is to journal your methods for correcting mistakes. Document your thought process and the steps you took, which will become an invaluable reference for future challenges, saving you significant time and effort. You can also use these ideas to help out your team or juniors when they face similar issues.

Additionally, learning from others' mistakes is equally important. During your scrum or team discussions, actively listen to the problems your colleagues face and how they resolve them. Take notes on their approaches, as there's a good chance you might encounter a similar issue in the future. By observing and absorbing lessons from both your experiences and those of others, you can build a strong foundation for continuous improvement and efficient problem-solving.

Exercise:

Document your and your co-worker's mistakes or errors that you encountered in your project and take corrective action(s).

	Errors or Mistake scenarios from you or co-worker	Preventive action	Learning	Can you share it to your team to help new members?
1				
2				
3				
4				
5				
6				
7				

Have an Open Mind:

As I mentioned several times earlier, keeping an open mind is crucial while solving a new problem or inventing something new. It will help you explore your thinking in multiple directions, and you might find various ways to approach a solution. It will help you find creative solutions. I have experienced this several times. I hope you will also find it!

9.4 Real-world Examples of Creative Solutions in Software Development

Looking at real-world examples, we will understand the importance of creativity and problem-solving techniques. Here, I am grabbing some examples demonstrating creative things and problem-solving ability in the real world, which we see daily.

a. Dropbox: Solving File Syncing Challenges

Earlier, people used to sync files across devices manually, which was cumbersome. File sharing became a problematic area for many users.

Creative Solution: Dropbox developed an innovative solution using cloud storage and synchronization algorithms. This solution allows users to sync files automatically across multiple devices and geographical locations. Although it looks simple, this solution has revolutionized file-sharing and backup systems.

Takeaway: Sometimes, Creativity is associated with simplifying complex problems for end users. You don't need to reinvent the wheel; instead, an innovative mindset that uses current technologies might suffice.

b. Slack: Simplified Team Communication

Earlier people used to use chat applications for internal communication within their team. Although they are helpful for communication, challenges arise when sharing data with one or many people in the group. Also, while discussing multiple topics, they must specify what topic they are talking about to ensure everything is clear.

Creative Solution: Slack created a unified solution combining chat and file-sharing applications and version control systems like GIT. It introduces new features that help create individual groups based on topics, teams, and projects, taking communication to the next level and pushing productivity.

Take Away: Creativity lies in combining existing technologies into a single platform, increasing organization productivity by simplifying workflows.

c. GitHub: Collaborative Platform for Coding

There are millions of developers worldwide, and coordinating code contributions is challenging. It leads to many conflicts and poor workflow.

Creative Solution: GitHub, a version control system, was created on top of GIT. It provides a user-friendly interface for distributed version control, collaboration, and branching and a public interface to pull code. It also provides an issue-tracking system and converts coding into a collaborative experience.

Take Away: Creativity lies in building a system streamlining collaboration in complex environments like software development.

d. Twitter: Scalability for Real-Time Communication

With its rise in popularity, Twitter faces challenges with increasing concurrent users, so scalability became an issue with a monolithic solution.

Creative Solution: Twitter migrated to microservice architecture, refactoring the product into independent, scalable, separately maintainable microservices. It allowed Twitter to handle a surge in traffic efficiently and made real-time communication very simple.

Take Away: Sometimes creativity involves re-architecture to solve scalability challenges while balancing simplicity with performance.

e. Netflix: Adoptive Streaming

Streaming high-definition content over an unstable internet connection is challenging, as users face disruptions that make streaming uncomfortable.

Creative Solution: Netflix developed the "Adoptive Streaming" technique, wherein if the internet speed degrades, the solution adjusts the video quality of streaming content in real time. This ensures that users will not be interrupted by the change in internet speed and can enjoy the content.

Takeaway: Creative solutions that optimize performance based on user conditions will improve the overall experience while maintaining accessibility.

Note: The above are just a few examples, but you can find many more in the software field. Feel free to explore as much as possible and get ideas during your free time.

The above examples show how software professionals can use creativity to overcome challenges, scale solutions, and transform industries.

9.5 Putting Creativity and Problem-Solving into Practice

Adopting creativity and problem-solving skills is a continuous process. The more you practice, the better you gain those skills and the more distinguished you become as a professional. Here are some tips that you can adopt for better growth:

Exercise:

- **Creative Learning Environment:** You should surround yourself with things that boost your creativity, such as books, online training resources, or conversations with colleagues. Learning should be your mantra; try to incorporate your learning into your work. If you don't get the opportunity to do so, apply for a side-line project. People can forget the technology(s) they learn if they don't practice it, so revise what you learn often.

- **Seeking feedback:** Feedback is one of the primary mechanisms by which anyone can improve their task. Creative thinking and problem-solving skills can be upskilled by regularly seeking inputs or feedback from peers, managers, or relevant people. It will help to understand how the thinking of others differs from your own thinking and provide food for analysis to fill the gap on why you did not think in that direction. Also, it will help you apply your thoughts on top of feedback ideas to arrive at a great solution. In this way, feedback helps improve your ideas and develops creative thinking.

- **Experiment with Tools**: Experiment with new tools and technologies, even if you feel uncomfortable. It will not only improve you but also boost your creativity. For example, you could try a new programming language, scripts, apps, developmental framework, and other relevant ones.

- **Practice Patience:** Creativity and problem-solving will take time, but don't get disheartened. It is common for people to take some time to find the right solution. It requires your dedicated, relentless, persevering efforts along with "patience." Believing in yourself will help develop patience. This patience will motivate you to put in continuous effort and help you overcome frustrations. Remember, overcoming challenges is as important as your end goal. It would help if you climbed (overcome) every minor step to reach the top.

Summary

- **Importance of Creativity**:

Creativity drives innovation in software development, impacting areas like architecture, bug fixing, automation, and project management. The chapter highlights a few real-world examples that depicting transformative role in problem-solving.

- **Techniques for Enhancing Creativity**:

    - **Mind Mapping**: Breaks complex problems into smaller and manageable tasks for better management.

    - **Brainstorming**: Encourages free-flowing ideas from every member without criticising anyone to foster innovation.

    - **Challenging Assumptions**: Promotes alternative solutions by rethinking established approaches.

- **Cross-Disciplinary Thinking**: Draws inspiration from other fields to innovate in software.

- **Taking Breaks**: Resting enhances productivity and creativity.

- **Collaboration**: Diverse perspectives lead to robust solutions.

- **Developing a Problem-Solving Mindset**:

  - Stay curious and seek the root causes of changes.

  - Embrace challenges with patience and perseverance.

  - Adopt structured thinking and scientific methods to resolve complex issues.

- **Real-Life Lessons**:

Examples of software professionals solving challenges creatively underline the importance of mindset in career growth.

Chapter 10

Building the Bridge to Success: Tracking Milestones and Metrics

"Success is the sum of small efforts, repeated day in and day out."

– Robert Collier

Until now, we have seen how to set our short—and long-term goals per our career vision. Once we set goals and start taking action on them, it is also essential to track them. You can construct success metrics for our actions. Metrics help us see where we currently stand and suggest if it requires any corrective action(s). Updating and monitoring your progress in the metrics daily will help you feel a sense of accomplishment and boost your confidence for tackling upcoming tasks.

This chapter will discuss how to track our progress towards our goals. It has three sections: Section 10.1 describes deep understanding and the definition of success. Section 10.2 describes a metrics board for monitoring growth, and section 10.3 discusses continuous improvement.

10.1 Defining Success in Your Software Career: What Does It Look Like?

Success in software has a broader meaning; it entirely depends on individuals. Everyone has their own view of success. For example, for interns, success is getting a full-time job; for software engineers, it may be getting promoted to senior with a hike; for tech leads, to become architects or managers, similarly in other domains. So, it is all about their aspirations. If you can define what is success for you, then it is easy to track your progress. Here are some tips on defining your success.

- Your success should align with personal and career aspirations, from a software developer to a software architect, project manager, engineering director and VP. Here, your success aligns with your career and personal aspirations. For example, You can define success as reducing 30 kg weight in the next 3 years. If you are overweight, this will align with your aspirations.

- Another meaningful way to define your success is by reflecting on a classic question often asked in HR interviews: *"Where do you see yourself in five or ten years?"* What kind of role do you aspire to? What impact do you hope to create? Answering this question can help you uncover your inner drivers—whether they lie in deepening your technical expertise, developing leadership and management capabilities, or inspiring and influencing others through your vision and actions (Gallo, 2011).

- Success can often be internal or external for individuals. Internal success is self-growth in a career, alignment of work towards career aspiration, and a sense of accomplishment. Conversely, salary hikes, work or office promotions, and rewards and recognitions indicate external success.

- As your career evolves, your definition of success must also change. For example, when you are a contract employee, your definition of success is to get a full-time position. After several years, when you are a director of engineering, your definition of success is to become a vice president or entrepreneur. It would help if you were flexible enough to change the definition of success regarding interests, skills, positions, or roles.

- Some core areas of success are *(1). technical expertise like mastery in modern programming languages, software architectures and even domain knowledge. (2). Leadership skills like team lead roles, mentoring and guiding projects and other developers. (3). Contribution to meaty projects or innovations that push you beyond technical boundaries.*

Exercise:

Define the meaning of "SUCCESS" in your words below:

____

____

____

____

____

____

____

Now as per the above data fill data below:

	Questionnaire	Yes or No	If No, then rewrite above as per success vision
1	Is your success is aligned with personal and career aspirations?		
2	Where do you want to see yourself after 5 years or 10 years?		
3	Do you think you will get both internal and external happiness if you work on your success?		
4	Are you regularly able to change the definition of success for short term stories?		

10.2 Building a Metrics Dashboard: Tools for Monitoring Growth

Till now, we have seen the definition of success. When do you start taking actions that are significant to monitor growth? The next question is how? It is through the metrics board.

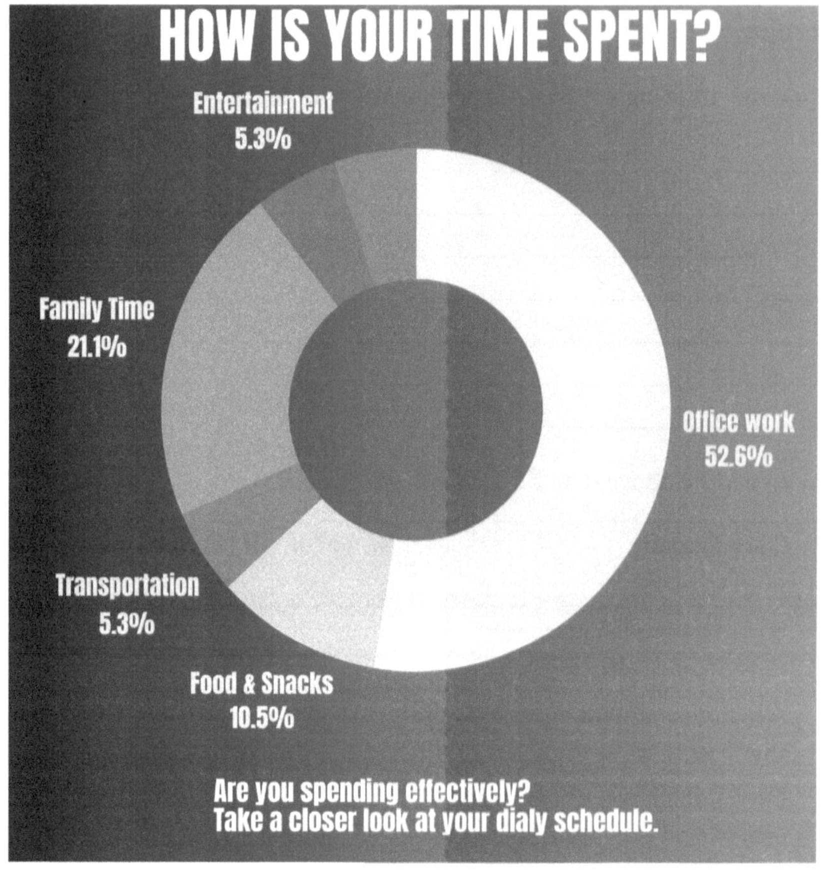

Figure 11.1: A Sample Metrics Dash Board for Daily Time

I hope you have seen railway stations or airports where you can see live tracking of time in which at what time the train or flight arrives or departs. It keeps on fluctuating until the train arrives. Your metrics board looks like that, and you can see your growth progress through the metrics board. Here, let us explore a few of the tools or dashboards to monitor your growth:

a. KPI (Key Performance Indicators):

We must identify key performance indicators defining our success. Some of the examples are:

- **Technical Skills**: learning modern programming languages, scripts, DevOps frameworks, frameworks, operating system(s), certifications or even contributions to open source projects.

- **Milestones**: number of skills acquired, projects completed, complex problems resolved or feature releases.

- **Leadership and Collaborations**: Number of projects led, mentorships, cross-functional work across groups or even customers

Note: Adapted from common industry practices in performance measurement.

Exercise:

Now fill in the table below based on your knowledge

	Technical Skills	Milestone Definition	Target Date for completion
1	Ex: Python Learning	Obtain Certification and Mini projects	In Next 6 months
2			
3			
4			
5			
6			

	Leadership and Collaborative Skills	Milestone Definition	Target Date for completion
1			
2			
3			
4			

b. Tracking tangible and non-tangible metrics:

Completing certifications, contributing to GitHub, growing in salary, holding job titles, and receiving feedback from peers are examples of tangible metrics.

Examples of intangible metrics are mental health, work-life balance, accomplishment satisfaction and, ideally, zero stress levels.

Tools: For professional growth, we can utilise online platforms such as **Udemy**, **Coursera**, and **LinkedIn Learning** as valuable training resources. We can use **JIRA, Trello, Asana**, or any other currently available tools to track our learning tasks. These tools help monitor the status of your tasks and track your progress.

For example, you planned to learn project management skills this year. First, identify the necessary skills for project management at a high level. Create a story for each of the skills in **JIRA** (you can also use other tools). Break each higher story into smaller, achievable tasks (sub-tasks). Set a timeline for each task and work on it every day. You can refer to **Udemy** or **LinkedIn** for resources for those skills. Align your JIRA tasks with the topics from the **Udemy** or LinkedIn courses you're learning, and follow a dedicated schedule to track your progress.

To improve productivity and to track milestones, we can use tools like **Notion, Evernote, or Todoist**. Tracking milestones will help you focus on your goals and complete your tasks. The usage of online tools makes your tracking smoother.

Lakshmi, a software professional, frequently uses the **Todoist** tool to track her learning milestones, particularly while studying automation with Python. When she began, she entered her learning goals and an estimated timeline into the tool. She updated her daily progress regularly and monitored it over time. As needed, she adjusted her goals based on her pace and progress. Finally, through consistent effort and tracking, she achieved her objective. The tool helped her stay focused and accountable throughout the journey.

Note: The tools and practices mentioned are inspired by widely used industry techniques for skill development and task tracking

Exercise:

	Identify your skill(s) to improve	Identify source to find resources to improve your skills	Identify a tool to map your skill to high level and low level stories	Identify tool to track your milestone
1				
2				
3				
4				

Visualisation: Visualization is a powerful technique for tracking progress. The contents of visualisation manifest in the form of graphs or pie charts. Individuals or even organisations use various tools to visualise work and growth progress. They often use online tools to track progress.

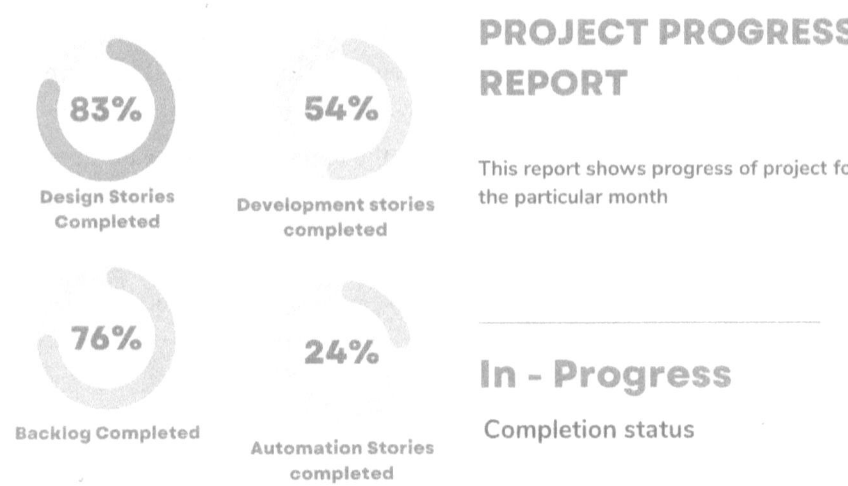

Figure 11.2: Sample Example of Visualisation of a development project

Retrospective Analysis: Conduct a retrospective visualisation of your daily, weekly, or bi-weekly metrics. Make any necessary adjustments to your actions. It will help you evaluate progress, adjust goals, and celebrate wins.

Adjust metrics: Each metric provides insights into your following actionable items. If you complete the current task, it is time to subscribe to new learnings, certifications, or projects.

Evolution: Metrics need to evolve according to your goals. As technology changes, your learning will also change. As the goal changes, update your metrics board as well.

Note: Inspired by Agile retrospectives and continuous improvement methodologies.

10.3 Reflecting and Iterating: The Importance of Continuous Improvement

As we discussed several times earlier, *learning, learning, and learning* should be our mantra. It emphasises continuous improvement. As we know, this software field is dynamic. Individuals emphasise their skills according to industry trends; reflection and iterations help us update our goals and strategies and stay current. Let's dive deep into reflection and iterations about our career progress.

Regular reflection: Set aside a dedicated time, say during Friday evening, Saturday morning, or whatever works for you, to reflect on your progress. During this process, you might probably have to ask a few questions like:

	Reflecting questions on your work	Action Items
1	What worked well over the last week?	
2	Are there any areas of improvement?	
3	What is my knowledge level over the previous week?	
4	Did I accomplish all my tasks effectively?	
5	Can I act on whatever I have learnt so far?	
6	If you complete some tasks, ask yourself what you need to learn next that aligns with your career aspiration?	
7	Are my aspirations completed?	

Iterating on Goals: The tech industry is incredibly dynamic, with today's technologies often becoming outdated within a few years. Updating existing systems and creating new ones must become routine with the progress of new inventions and innovations. It is vital to have an eye on upcoming technologies. Revisiting your goals regularly and adjusting based on changing circumstances is vital. Reflect on whether your current interests align with the goals you previously set, and consider the latest job market trends. For example, you might initially aim to master the JAVA programming language. Still, if you later discover a stronger demand for Python in the job market, shifting your focus to learning Python would be wise.

Realising from Mistakes: Setbacks are very common for software professionals, irrespective of positions, domains, or experience levels. The main thing here is how you overcome failures. Consider this an opportunity for learning and a stepping stone to reaching your final goal.

Exercise:

	Setbacks	How to Overcome from Setbacks
1		
2		
3		
4		

Feedback: Seek regular feedback from peers, mentors, managers, and some seniors in your network. It will help you correct continuously, develop skills, and improve performance.

Adjustable Metrics: Your metrics should be flexible enough to accommodate new KPIs and modify existing KPI parameters. For example, once your metrics track strategic thinking, you should incorporate learning communication skills. In short, your metrics need to be dynamic.

Long-term Iterations: Continuous improvement is not limited to a shorter period. It is about long-term accomplishments, and because of the dynamic nature of the software industry, this might require a career. So, regular iterations are needed to ensure our learning path meets modern trends.

Growth Mindset: Embrace a Carol's growth mindset that sees challenges as opportunities to learn new things. Continuously seek or discover new ways to refine your skills, approaches, and strategies for success.

Celebrating Progress: Continuous improvement also emphasises celebrating even minor successes, which boosts our confidence in performing our work and motivates us.

Note: The above concepts reflect common industry best practices for continuous learning and career growth.

Summary

This chapter helps build a bridge to destined success and tracks your progress towards success. It starts by clarifying individual success and effective methods to track your journey towards success, like metrics dashboards, and highlights the importance of continuous improvement.

- Success varies from person to person and evolves. For some, it means landing a full-time role; for others, it means stepping into leadership positions like architects or managers. Success can be internal, such as achieving growth and fulfilment, or external, like receiving promotions or recognition. Defining success requires aligning our personal and professional goals, clearly understanding what drives you, and adjusting your focus as your career progresses. Some of the fundamental components of success are developing technical expertise, leadership abilities and making meaningful contributions.

- Progress tracking requires following structured metrics. Here, you can use them. Dashboards or tools like key performance indicators (KPIs), tangible metrics like obtaining certification and actions, and intangible factors like work-life balance help measure growth. Tools like JIRA and Todoist, visualization, and regular review enable professionals to monitor progress effectively. Also, they can make necessary adjustments to reach their goals efficiently.

- Continuous improvement is essential in a constantly evolving industry. Regular reflection, feedback, and iterative goal-setting ensure alignment with career aspirations and market demands. Celebrating small wins boosts confidence and keeps motivation high.

- This chapter provides practical methods and insights to help professionals bridge the gap between their standards and aspirations.

Chapter 11

Harvesting the Fruits of Success: The Role of Recognition in the Software World

Generally, we can harvest fruits only after they have ripened, due to the prolonged effort of farmers from sowing seeds. It is a metaphor I used, wherein, after the successful completion of projects, people who performed well will be rewarded, irrespective of their positions, roles, experiences, or domains. Similarly, when you accomplish your goals, you need to celebrate the achievement. Recognition plays a unique role in motivating people to perform upcoming tasks. It also gives a sense of accomplishment, satisfaction, happiness, and pride. Additionally, they utilise social media platforms to share their recognition with friends and their network. It will also enhance your profile.

In this chapter, let's explore the role of recognition on individuals. This chapter contains three sections. Section 1 discusses recognising milestones and celebrating achievements in the tech world. Section 2 emphasises recognising recognition culture in the IT field, and Chapter 3 builds on reflection on accomplishments.

11.1 Why We Need to Recognize Milestones and Celebrate Achievements in Tech World

Milestones act as checkpoints for various accomplishments. Every goal you set should align with your milestone. So, it is essential to recognise milestones to maintain momentum and moral values. Here are a few examples of milestones:

- Mastering Python programming with real-world projects.

- Promoted as Senior Software Architect.

- Obtaining Certification in Cloud Computing.

a) Why We Need to Acknowledge Milestones

Here, we can find details on why we need to acknowledge milestones.

a. Celebrations:

Every time we accomplish a target, we need to make sure to celebrate. It need not be grand, but a small outing with family members or friends, such as a gathering sharing success stories, often gives new energy and happiness. What I experienced is that if someone says, "Good job !!" with a smile, it motivates me to try new things. These small moments of celebration build confidence and help us recharge for future work. As James Clear explains in *Atomic Habits* (2018), every time we celebrate a win—no matter how small—it reinforces the identity we're trying to build. So, when you complete something meaningful, please take a moment to mark it. You're not just enjoying the moment—you're strengthening your mindset and motivation for what's next.

b. Motivational Boost:

Recognition has a direct connection to motivation. It gives us that inner feeling of, "Yes, I did it!"—which pushes us to aim higher the next time. When we acknowledge these milestones, we create a loop of continuous improvement. In *The Progress Principle*, Amabile and Kramer (2011) discuss how small wins can spark joy, engagement, and creativity in our work. Even simple recognition can make a big difference. Similarly, Daniel Pink in *Drive* (2009) explains that progress and mastery are key ingredients for intrinsic motivation. That's why, when we take time to acknowledge our achievements, we're not just celebrating—we're preparing ourselves mentally for even greater challenges ahead.

Exercise:

Does you acknowledge your milestones? If so, how?

____

____

b) Psychological Impacts

a. Productivity Booster:

In my software journey, I've seen this—when people are recognised, something changes inside them. Some positive energy in them. They begin to take real ownership. It's not just about doing prescribed work, but also about adding more value to tasks; that responsibility turns into energy. Of course, several times, I too felt the same way, wherein I could see an elevation in productivity level.

b. Job Satisfaction:

I've observed that when leadership genuinely values someone's contribution, it has a profound impact. The person starts to feel proud, not just about what they have delivered, but also about who they are becoming. Their job no longer feels like a routine—it feels meaningful. And that meaning builds stability. I've seen teammates including myself take bold steps in life, like buying a home or planning for their future, simply because they felt secure and appreciated at work. That's the level of confidence real recognition can build.

c. Improved Team Cohesion:

Recognition never stops with just the individual—it always ripples through the team. When one person is celebrated, others feel inspired. It builds a quiet sense of healthy competition and a loud sense of unity. I've been part of teams where we openly appreciated each other's wins—those teams communicated better, trusted each other more, and delivered stronger results. The atmosphere becomes positive, focused, and driven. In such spaces, people push their limits and still enjoy the journey.

In short:

Celebrating milestones is not just about good vibes. It directly fuels personal growth, strengthens teams, and uplifts the entire project. While everything I've shared is from real project life, it also echoes the ideas found in books like *The Progress Principle* and *Drive*—both of which delve deeply into how recognition and small wins create a lasting impact.

11.2 Reflecting on Achievements: Fuelling Motivation for Future Success

Celebrations are not merely for enjoying, feeling proud and then forgetting; they fuel your motivation to do your best. You might have seen reward certificates mentioning "best wishes", which means your success is not limited to the present time; it needs to extend to future work. Reflection plays a unique role in achieving success. That is the primary purpose of the award. In this section, we examine how to reflect on our accomplishments.

The Role of Reflection in Career Growth

Reflecting on achievements helps in self-assessments. It allows individuals to track their professional or personal growth. It will help to understand individual strengths and, of course, areas for improvement. Additionally, it is helpful to know the amount of contribution individuals have made to the projects they worked on.

Another crucial point that reflecting on achievement helps with is a growth mindset. As we have seen, achievements lead to celebration, which internally increases motivation and focus on the work. Reflecting on achievement will also help with continuous learning, raise curiosity, and help treat challenges as learning opportunities for upcoming work.

Using Celebrations as Motivation for Future Challenges

As we saw in the previous point, celebration leads to motivation, which in turn helps us face future challenges. The moment you get motivated, it opens doors for upcoming work. Groupwise or teamwise, celebration helps to set ambitious but achievable goals. It also fosters continuous improvement and learning.

Summary

Recognition's Importance:

- Acts as a motivational boost,

- Fostering happiness, pride, and satisfaction.

- Enhances individual profiles via acknowledgement shared on social platforms.

Acknowledging Milestones:

- Celebrating milestones boosts a)morale, b)confidence, and c) productivity.

- Psychological benefits include:

    o Improved job satisfaction,

    o Team cohesion

    o Individual ownership.

Reflecting on Achievements:

- Enables self-assessment, highlights strengths, and fosters a growth mindset.

- Celebrations fuel motivation for future challenges, fostering a positive team environment.

- Practical steps include regular reflection meetings, agile retrospectives, and milestone-based celebrations.

Overall recognition, reflection, and celebration drive motivation and success in the software world.

Chapter 12

Navigating Career Transitions and Growth Opportunities

In the private sector, career transitions are widespread. The fast-growing and dynamic software industry is no different from that. Growth opportunities will reach individuals as the experience grows and exhibits outstanding performance. It is up to the individual to take it and move ahead. Most of the individuals will transition to new roles. Some individuals move across groups in the same or different organisations to explore new environments or technologies. For individuals who are not comfortable with project work, the environment, or monetary compensation, it is pronounced for them to pursue outside work.

Hence, transitions depend purely on individual interests or requirements. Sometimes, the question arises: What strategies must we follow to pursue career transitions and growth opportunities? This chapter will discuss a few methods for managing career changes, explain how applying the growth mindset can make transitions smoother, and outline how to plan long-term career development and advancement.

12.1 Strategies for Managing Career Changes and New Opportunities

Career changes will be challenging because of the many unknowns, but they will also be exciting. Whether you are shifting into a new role within your current company, moving to a different organisation, or switching career paths, you must be prepared for the Blackbox. Here are some strategies to help you navigate these transitions smoothly.

Embrace Change with an Open Mindset

A career change can intimidate you as you will need a clearer picture of the nature of work, colleagues or teams, supervisors, job stability, growth, etc. But it would help if you remembered that you were one of many who embraced this change. So, approach the Change with an open mindset. Apply the growth mindset principle, like treating the Change as a new learning opportunity. As I mentioned earlier, the role you will perform today will be part of your resume in future; the skills that you acquire with the new role will make your resume eye-catching, so embrace change with a healthy mindset. You need to believe the role will give you an immense opportunity to learn and grow.

Research information and make preparation

Before you step into a new role or organisation, make sure to build a strong foundation, just like how you wouldn't cross a river without first checking the depth of the water. Career transitions require thoughtful preparation before you dive into them. Start by researching the skills they're looking for, the kind of expectations the role demands, and the kind of environment you're stepping into.

During interviews, speak with honesty and clarity. Try to understand not just the role, but also what kind of person the company is looking for. If you're too eager, be cautious—express your interests wisely. Sometimes, when your aspirations don't align with the company's direction, it can work against you. So ask: What is the interview process like? What products do they build? What technologies are in use? Who are the people you might work with? If you're moving across organisations, check how current employees feel about their work and the team culture. But take their opinions with perspective—everyone's experience is different. No place is perfect. There will always be trade-offs—whether it's the technology, team dynamics, growth opportunities, or work-life balance. The key is to decide what you're willing to compromise on and what's non-negotiable for you.

As *Chamorro-Premuzic and Yearsley (2017)* write in *Harvard Business Review*, "the best job on paper" isn't always the right one. Long-term happiness often stems from working in an environment that aligns with your personal values and work style. In the end, it's not just about where you go—it's about whether that place feels right for who you are becoming.

Career experts from platforms like *LinkedIn Learning* and *Indeed* also recommend preparing thoroughly, understanding the required skills, the company's mission, the technologies in use, and the team structure. With greater clarity, you will become more confident and your actions will be more purposeful.

LinkedIn Learning. (n.d.). *Career development and transition planning.* Indeed Career Guide. (n.d.). *How to research a company before applying.*

Doing this groundwork can help you make informed decisions and prepare effectively for interviews. It could include learning new technologies, understanding different company cultures, or familiarising yourself with the role's responsibilities or monetary compensation.

Build a Support Network

With the support network, you can receive help with introductions, encouragement, better insights into the role, high-level product familiarisation, simplified internal and external communication on projects, and all other necessary resources to smooth your transition and ensure a successful completion.

Career transitions can often feel like walking through a foggy forest—you may know the destination, but the path is unclear. In such times, a well-built professional network becomes your compass. As highlighted in an article by *Cross and Thomas (2011) in Harvard Business Review*, the most successful professionals don't just build large networks—they make smart ones. These networks include people who offer internal referrals, hidden opportunities, practical guidance, and most importantly, emotional support. They energise you, provide clarity during uncertain moments, and walk beside you as you navigate new terrain. Your support network isn't just about who you know—it's about who strengthens you when the journey gets tough.

Here are a few steps to build a support system in your profession:

- **Mentorship** - The Mentor will provide proper guidance, which will ultimately lead to success.

- **Join a professional forum** – It will help you develop a network and find broad support.

- **Connect with Colleagues** – It will broaden your sources of help and build meaningful professional relationships.

- **Offering Help** – Offering help to colleagues helps build confidence and foster a healthy relationship.

- **Keep in touch** – If someone in your organisation whom you know leaves, or whenever you change organisation, make sure you connect with them virtually. With that, you can still reach out to them and pave the way to your success.

Martin recently joined a software engineer at a tech company. He needs to receive strong support from his network to succeed in his job and advance in his career. He did the following things:

- He requested that senior member Debasish be his mentor. They set up regular meetings. Debasish helped Martin find solutions to tricky coding problems and provided him with career advice.

- He introduced himself to colleagues, attended regular team meetings, and participated in group conversations over instant messenger. He became familiar with them and developed a good understanding of them. Eventually, he became accustomed to receiving the necessary assistance from team members.

- He joined the company's technical knowledge-sharing forums, where people shared ideas and thoughts on various scenarios. Debasish used to understand many things from forums.

- Debasish often helps juniors settle and is used to sharing much learning. It allows him to win their confidence and develop good relationships with the team.

- He would regularly contact his mentors, colleagues, and manager. He was also part of his colleague's success, building strong employee relationships.

So, with his positive attitude, Debasish built a strong network with his peers, mentor(s), and manager, became part of a technical forum, helped others, and was regularly in touch. It helped him learn, grow, and excel in the job.

Be Flexible and Adaptable

Being more flexible and adaptable during career transition is essential in the fast-paced tech world. It would help if you were open to any challenge. Flexibility can include learning a new programming language, adjusting to a different management style, work culture, work environment, project setup, other team members, various types of work, technology, process, style, etc. Whatever the condition, the ability to adapt to the current environment helps you succeed.

Set Goals

As we know from earlier chapters, goal setting is essential to achieving anything. Career transition is no different. You need to set clear-cut goals to have a purpose and a sense of direction to progress in your career. It will help to stay focused during the transition period. Consider what you want to achieve in your new role or opportunity and break those goals into smaller, actionable steps or tasks.

Roopa, the HR assistant in a software company, is transitioning from an HR assistant to a recruitment specialist. To smoothen the transition process, she set goals using Doran's S.M.A.R.T. framework for the topics: improve turnaround time for hiring, improve hiring quality, enhance candidate experience, expand recruitment channels, reduce cost-to-hire, etc. Roopa started taking action and tracking progress often, which helped her achieve goals and the organisation. So, setting goals helps to motivate individuals and offers a roadmap for execution.

12.2 Applying Mindset Principles to Handle Transitions Smoothly

How you transition your career solely depends on your mindset. The right attitude can turn a potentially stressful experience into a positive and empowering one. Let's explore how to apply mindset principles to navigate career changes more smoothly.

Adopt a Growth Mindset

In earlier chapters, we've already discussed the power of a growth mindset—how tuning your mindset can help you achieve remarkable things. This mindset also plays a crucial role during career transitions. Instead of viewing *challenges* in a new role as *obstacles*, you begin to see them as *stepping stones*. You start adapting to new responsibilities and technologies, building strong *work relationships* with peers, mentors, and supervisors, embracing the ideas behind products, participating in organisational forums, and getting comfortable with new tools and methodologies. All of this creates a *solid foundation* to excel in your new role.

Carol Dweck, in her book *Mindset: The New Psychology of Success* (2006), emphasises that people with a growth mindset view challenges as chances to grow rather than threats. They don't worry about exposing weaknesses, but they welcome the opportunity to learn and improve. This kind of mindset is essential when navigating change and learning in a new role. I have experienced this a few times in my career.

Annie, a business analyst at a software company, is *transitioning* to a senior business analyst position in another organisation. Although challenging, she adopted growth mindset principles, wherein she took *ownership of learning* by enrolling in an advanced course(s) on digital transformation at Udemy. Additionally, she seeks *regular feedback* from peers and technical teams, adopting their strategies instead of trying to go it alone. She *reframes* mistakes during the project as *new learning opportunities*, analyses how each setback improves her abilities, and *mentors* junior analysts. She also used her current project as a learning opportunity. So with a growth mindset, she was able to make a smooth transition.

View Transitions as Learning Opportunities

In 2013, I made a significant career transition—from a mobile application developer to a software developer in the telecom domain. The telecom domain was entirely new to me, and I was initially overwhelmed by the complexity of its technologies and systems. I had moments of doubt about my decision and felt deeply uncomfortable at times.

However, I gradually began to understand the immense value of the technology I was working with. I soon realised this transition was a golden opportunity to align my career with emerging trends. I adopted a growth mindset and nurtured a strong belief in my ability to learn. Step by step, I adapted to the new environment.

I used to get help from my mentor whenever I needed it, and I sincerely thank him from the bottom of my heart for his unwavering support. I invested time in learning the fundamentals of telecom. Additionally, I viewed each challenge as a gateway for growth. Over time, I not only became comfortable with the technology but also began making meaningful contributions to the project. That became the starting point for future opportunities. This experience taught me a powerful lesson: **career transitions are not setbacks—they are gateways to growth and new possibilities.**

Stay Resilient

Never think a career transition is a cakewalk. You can expect setbacks as well. Whether you struggle to adjust to a new role and technologies, face rejection in the job market, or deal with unexpected obstacles, it is most important to remain *resilient*. It is the ability of an individual or group to counteract the situation, a skill you can/need to develop over time.

The American Psychological Association (2022) defines resilience as the ability to adapt well in the face of adversity, trauma, tragedy, or significant stress. This psychological strength is key to enduring and growing through career transitions (APA, 2022).

When things don't go as planned, like if a layoff occurs, here are the steps which we can follow:

Handling job loss

- **Digest the News-** It's natural to feel upset when you lose your job. But take a deep breath—stay calm and focus on what needs your attention. Remind yourself: *"I am not the first person who got laid off. It is just a phase. It will pass."* If needed, reach out to family members or friends for emotional support.

- **Understand the Benefits -** Take time to review the benefits you're eligible for from your former employer—final paycheck(salary slip), insurance coverage, severance, etc. Ensure you claim everything on time. Follow up politely if something is delayed.

- **Support Your Family -** Reassure your family. Let them know you have the talent and knowledge to land another job. Help them stay calm by projecting confidence and a positive attitude.

- **Practice Meditation** - To maintain mental and emotional balance, incorporate meditation into your daily routine. If you're new to it, seek guidance from online resources and meditation experts.

- **Sharpen Your Skills** - Revisit your previous projects, review notes you took at work, and practice the skills listed on your resume. Leverage online platforms to upskill yourself and ensure they align with what you are looking for in your future job. Gain hands-on experience with the new skills by working on projects that utilise those skills.

- **Update Your Resume with the Latest Experience** - Craft a compelling resume that reflects your strengths and recent experience. Seek feedback from professionals in your domain. Tailor your resume for each opportunity to capture recruiters' attention.

- **Update Your Social Media Profile** - If you have already created a profile on social media platforms like LinkedIn, update it with your new skills and projects. Try to get endorsement from your former colleagues on your skills.

- **Apply for Jobs** - Actively apply through job portals like LinkedIn and other relevant platforms in your region. While LinkedIn is widely used globally, consider exploring local platforms that are popular in your country as well.

- **Get Support From Your Network** - Reach out to professionals you trust in your network. Share your situation honestly and request support—whether it's referrals, guidance, or job leads. Most people are willing to help when you ask sincerely.

- **Avoid Procrastination** - It's easy to get distracted or demotivated, but remember: the sooner you act, the faster you'll find your next role. Be proactive. Your motto should be: *"Get hired as early as possible."*

- **Stabilise Your Finances** - Assess Your Current Financial Situation. Minimise expenses, cancel unnecessary subscriptions, and keep only those that add value to your job search and learning.

- **Prioritise Health** - Take care of your health—physical, mental, and emotional. Avoid unproductive conversations or stress-inducing environments. Stay calm, focused, and optimistic.

- **Believe in Yourself** - A strong belief system will carry you through tough times. Use affirmations, express gratitude, and visualise your success. Train your subconscious mind to stay positive and take action.

- **Create a Clear Plan** - Define Your Path Forward. What skills should you reinforce? What new areas should you explore? What kind of roles are you targeting? Use SMART goals (explained earlier in this book) and track your daily progress.

- **Interviews** - Never ignore recruiter calls. Follow up after each interview. And when you attend interviews, don't dwell on the job loss—show energy, confidence, and clarity like you always have.

Note: For interview steps section 13.4 Interview tips to improve chance of hiring

Practice Self-Reflection

As discussed in earlier chapters, practising self-reflection is also essential during a career transition. Self-reflection is a core part of experiential learning models such as *Kolb's (1984)*, which emphasize learning from experience through reflection. Please take time to reflect on your strengths and areas of improvement. Ask yourself questions like:

- What do I gain from this transition?

- What challenges do I expect to face, and how can I prepare for them?

- How can I apply my existing skills in this new role?

Reflecting on these questions helps you stay grounded and better prepared for the journey ahead.

Emma has been promoted from a software developer to a team lead in a software company. Although she was excited, she needed more certainty in managing people. *She practices Self-Reflection.* After the first month, Emma reflects on her experience by asking herself the following:

- "How well am I supporting my team?"

- "Am I developing leadership qualities?"

- "What feedback I am getting from my team members?"

- "Is my work adding value to my experience? if yes, in what way?"

- "Am I giving sufficient time for self-learning?"

Emma notices that while she's good at solving technical issues, she needs to improve her communication skills to provide better guidance to her team. This self-reflection leads her to attend *leadership training* and set personal goals for being a more approachable leader.

Maintain a Positive Attitude

Irrespective of the situation, being positive will always help you get motivated. It will help you re-energise and push you to work towards your goal. It also enables you to focus and open up to new opportunities. Even during difficult circumstances like recessions, layoffs, and project uncertainty, staying optimistic will keep individuals calm and focus on the goals to be accomplished. A positive mindset will make the transition easier and make you more resilient in the face of future challenges.

12.3 Plan Your Long-Term Career Advancement

Career transition is not a short-term process. You need to consider long-term career growth and advancement in your professional life. Let's discuss a few strategies for advancing in our careers.

Set Long-Term Career Goals

Every software professional needs to have a vision for long-term career goals. Technology changes every year, and the number of professionals in the software industry is increasing; you need to visualize where you stand after a long time, in the next five, ten, or even twenty years, concerning technology, skills, position, stability and even assets or wealth. So, every professional needs to have a long-term career developmental vision board, which starts with setting clear goals. What roles do you aspire to? What skills do you need to develop to get there?

Start by defining your ultimate career goals and break them into smaller, achievable action items. For example, if you want to become a software architect, your short-term goals include gaining expertise in system design, leading large projects, and learning advanced programming techniques.

Chiamaka, a senior manager, aspires to become an entrepreneur. She must set short—and long-term business goals to develop the skillset, network, and mindset required for success.

To achieve her mission, she set short-term goals for half a year to two, like developing a business idea, building essential skills required for business, coming up with a business plan, developing a network and seeking mentors, securing initial investment, testing the business idea with the minimum viable product before scaling. For the long-term goal for three to five years, she set goals like scaling a business, diversifying revenue sources or streams, establishing a solid brand, planning financial independence, establishing a brand, building a legacy, becoming an industry leader, etc. After that, she started working on the action items she planned. She gets motivated daily by looking at her vision board and goals and working to accomplish them.

Long-term goals provide direction and motivation, guiding your career decisions and helping you stay on track.

Continuously Develop Your Skills

No software professional can afford to say, "*I know a few skills; that's enough to survive my lifetime!*" If you're thinking that way, let me tell you—you're playing a risky game. The software industry is dynamic, fast-paced, and ever-evolving. Things are changing every single day—from tools and technologies to roles and responsibilities. You need to stay **hungry to learn**, adapt, and grow with the wave.

That means investing in your education—attending tech conferences, acquiring new certifications, watching tutorials, and staying current with industry trends. Yes, technical skills matter—but they are **not the whole story**. Leadership, communication, resilience, problem-solving, and emotional intelligence—these are the **real differentiators** that will push you ahead in your career marathon.

Even the **World Economic Forum's Future of Jobs Report** (2023) strongly backs this, highlighting that the most in-demand skills by 2027 won't just be about code. Skills such as **analytical thinking, creativity, emotional resilience, leadership**, and **technological agility** will drive success. Therefore, continuous upskilling is **no longer an option—it's a matter of survival and success combined.**(World Economic Forum, 2023).

Build a Professional Network

Your career growth requires a well-defined professional network. Building and maintaining good relationships with colleagues, peers, and mentors can open doors to new opportunities, whether job offers, mentorship, or valuable advice. We can regularly interact with professionals from current organisations and other organisations across the globe. Different platforms are available to achieve this, such as LinkedIn, Meetup, Behance, Wellfound, GitHub, etc. Today, the most popular platform for professional networking and job searching is LinkedIn. Most of you have built a network on LinkedIn or other sites.

If you have not done so, I request that you start today. I also recommend attending industry events, joining professional groups, and trying to connect with others in your field. Your network can provide support during transitions and help you advance in your career.

Seek Out Growth Opportunities

To achieve a long-term career, seeking growth opportunities is essential. You can achieve this through:

Work on side-line projects to practice new skills you have learned and experiment with the latest technologies.

- volunteering for challenging projects.

- ask for constructive feedback from your peers, supervisors, mentors, and professional mates, like those you worked with earlier.

- advance your skills by attending workshops, courses or even certifications;

- pursue networking opportunities by attending conferences, seminars, and network events to meet new people,

- take leadership roles by taking small initiatives, and even if you don't have skills

- exchange thoughts or opinions with professionals and enlighten yourself to stay updated with modern trends.

By being proactive and seeking growth opportunities, you'll gain experience and demonstrate a willingness to take on new challenges. It will build your skills and position you for future promotions or career advancements.

Balance Your Short-Term and Long-Term Goals

We need to remember that short-term goals help you achieve long-term goals. So, it is vital to strike a balance between these two that allows you to continue growing while performing well in your current role.

For example, while you work toward long-term career development, ensure you excel in your current job by delivering high-quality work. Also, build strong relationships with your team and contribute to the company's success. Balancing these two ensures you're progressing in your career without neglecting your responsibilities.

Regularly Evaluate and Adjust Your Career Plan

Your career plan is not set in stone—it should evolve as you gain new experiences and encounter different opportunities. Regularly evaluate your growth progress and adjust your goals as necessary. What might have been your dream job a few years ago could change as you grow and learn more about yourself.

Being flexible and open to new possibilities allows you to adapt your career plan to fit your evolving interests and the ever-changing job market.

12.4 Interview tips to improve chance of hiring

The following tips are based on my personal experience attending and mentoring others through job interviews. They are practical suggestions and not tied to any specific research.

- **Career Gap – Be Prepared:** If you have a career gap, expect to be asked about it. Be honest, confident, and positive in your response. Emphasise that you stayed engaged with your skills during the gap—mention any projects, online courses, freelance work, or repositories (GitHub, portfolio sites) you worked on. The goal is to assure them you weren't idle.

- **Show a Positive Attitude -** Your behaviour plays a significant role in achieving interview success. Stay upbeat, genuinely express interest in the role, and convey enthusiasm. When discussing their company or product, show genuine curiosity—ask relevant questions and demonstrate that you genuinely care.

- **Stay Calm – Don't Panic.** You don't need to answer every question perfectly. It's okay to miss a few—most interviewers are satisfied if you perform well on 70–80% of the questions. Stay composed and avoid showing frustration or nervousness on your face.

- **Don't Give Up Midway - Interviewers Respect Perseverance.** If you don't know the exact answer, try to reason your way through it logically based on your experience. Even partial answers show that you're thinking. Remember, the interview ends when the interviewer says so—stay engaged until the end.

- **Take Your Time – Don't Rush** - When asked to solve a coding or logic problem, don't dive in immediately. Clarify the question by asking follow-up questions to ensure a complete understanding of the problem. Even if your initial solution is not perfect, it shows your thought process. Then iterate and improve.

- **Learn from Failure** - Many people don't clear interviews on their first attempt. If you fail, don't feel discouraged. Take notes on the questions asked, reflect on your answers, and use the experience to prepare better for the next one.

- **Maintain Smile and Energy** - A positive demeanour can go a long way. Maintain a gentle smile and steady energy throughout the interview—it builds rapport and leaves a positive impression.

- **Have an Open Mind** - Approach the interview with an open mind. Flexibility in thinking helps you tackle unexpected or complex questions calmly and creatively.

- **Check Your Infrastructure (for Online Interviews)** - Ensure your laptop, internet connection, webcam, and microphone are all in good condition. Test them before the interview to avoid last-minute issues.

- **Eat Before the Interview** - Have a light meal at least 30 minutes before the interview. It helps maintain energy and focus, especially for more extended or technical interviews.

- **Follow Up After the Interview** - After the interview, don't hesitate to follow up with HR or the recruiter. A polite follow-up shows professionalism and interest in the role.

Summary

Career transition is crucial for every software professional, whether within or outside an organisation. It offers opportunities to grow and advance in our careers. This chapter focuses on practical strategies and mindsets required for smoother career transitions within and outside the organisation.

Proper preparation and the ability to adapt to any environment are key factors. The chapter discusses the importance of having the right mindset and being willing to learn new things. When considering transition, it is essential to research new roles, properly understand requirements or expectations, and seek guidance from mentors. Adaptability to new environments and roles and setting clear-cut goals are essential for a successful transition.

The chapter highlights how career change is an opportunity to grow and learn in the software world, and with new roles and responsibilities, one can advance in one's career. It demonstrates overcoming challenges such as rejection by staying resilient and continuously learning, cementing and developing professional networks, and maintaining a constructive outlook. Few stories or illustrations help us understand how setbacks can be transformed into growth opportunities and success.

The chapter explains the importance of self-reflection and illustrates how it is an essential tool for evaluating our strengths and identifying areas for improvement. By adapting these principles or ideas, professionals can improve their transition.

Ultimately, staying proactive and optimistic ensures that career changes become opportunities for personal and professional development, paving the way for long-term success.

Chapter 13

The Ritual Algorithm: Programming Success into Your Life

Productive habits are essential for every software professional(in fact, every human being) to lead healthy and happy lives in both professional and personal life. Developing productive habits and routines is essential for creating a positive mindset, boosting productivity, and achieving a healthy work-life balance.

The next question is how we can build productive habits? In this chapter, we will discuss building habits that support a *positive* attitude, establishing effective routines to *enhance productivity* and *balance*, and using *tools and strategies* to maintain these habits.

13.1 Building Daily Habits that Support a Positive Mindset

A *positive mindset* can significantly impact your personal and professional life. It will help to avoid/minimize anxiety and stress. Developing *daily habits* that foster positivity and resilience can help you approach challenges with a constructive attitude. Here's how to build habits that support a positive mindset:

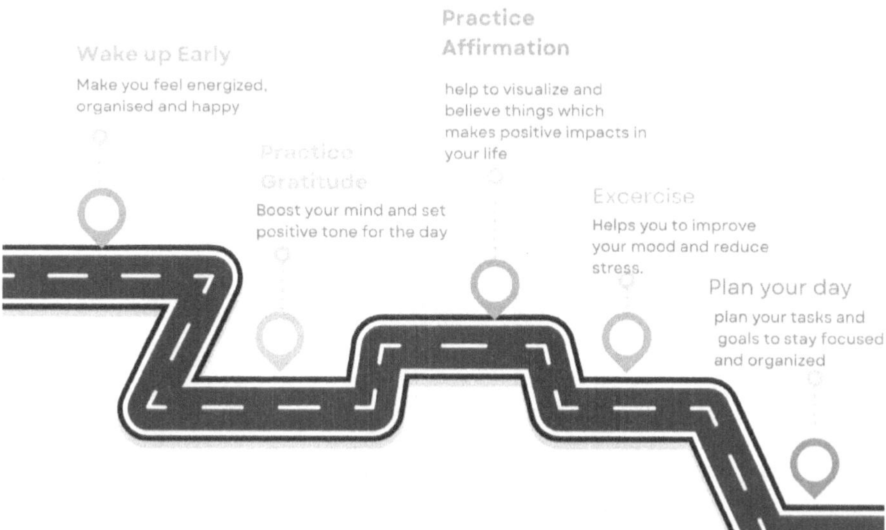

Figure 13.1: Daily Habits for Positive Mindset

Wake Up Early:

Start your day early to give yourself time to prepare and avoid rushing. Waking up early can help you feel more energized, organized and less stressed. My recommendation is to wake up at least by 5:00 a.m. every day.

Figure 13.2: Wake up early

I know it will be challenging initially, but after a week, you will feel better, and you can experience magic over time. In my experience, waking up is a mammoth task if you sleep less than 8 hours. Otherwise, it is a cakewalk after the first week of the start.

Practice Gratitude:

Gratitude is all about feeling **thankful** towards people, situations, education, institutions, and even the little things that have touched your life, directly or indirectly. It's a beautiful feeling of appreciation for everything that has shaped you.

Every morning, take a quiet moment to reflect on what you're grateful for. Say "thank you" in your mind or heart—to the divine, your body, your health, your peace of mind, your mindset, your gurus (teachers), parents, spouse, children, food, water, friends, your organization or university, your work, your teammates, your supervisors, your salary, savings, assets—and the list goes on. You'll slowly begin to notice how much you are already blessed with.

This simple practice sets a powerful tone for the day. It helps to:

a) calm your mind, b) uplift your spirit, and c) see the good that already exists. When you practice gratitude regularly, it can reduce stress, improve emotional well-being, and build your mental resilience.

As researchers Emmons and McCullough (2003) found, *gratitude* has the power to enhance your overall well-being and help you remain **resilient** during challenging times.

Practice Affirmation:

An **affirmation** is a positive statement that you repeat to yourself to build confidence, stay motivated, and shift your mindset in a better direction. It's like giving your mind a daily dose of encouragement—especially useful when you're feeling stuck or doubtful.

By saying affirmations regularly, for example: *"I am learning and growing every day"* or *"I handle challenges with confidence"*—you are slowly training your mind to believe in your strengths and potential. Over time, these repeated positive thoughts begin to influence your actions.

Studies have shown that affirmations can reduce stress, enhance emotional resilience, and foster a healthier, more resilient mindset. They help you stay grounded in your values, especially during challenging situations (Sherman & Cohen, 2006).

Thanks to my guru, *Dr. Manjunath*, for guiding me into the beautiful habit of practising affirmations daily. His words truly shaped my routine and mindset. As per his advice, I recorded affirmations in my voice, and when I started listening to them every day, I began to feel a shift in my thoughts, energy, and even how I approached challenges. I follow his guidance by practising affirmations early in the morning before starting my day, and again at night before going to sleep. While doing this, I gently close my eyes and visualise as if my goal has already been accomplished. The key lesson I learned is: your actions must align with your affirmations. Just saying them isn't enough—you must take action with faith, effort, and consistency to see results.

Here are some powerful affirmation examples:

"I attract positive energy from the universe and am surrounded by it."

"Every challenge I face opens the door to personal and professional growth."

"Every day, I shape my body and feel confident, energetic, and powerful."

"I maintain healthy and meaningful relationships with everyone I meet."

"I tackle problems confidently, and the right ideas come to me when I need them."

"I always engage in healthy, productive discussions that benefit both me and those around me."

"I radiate positivity and inspire others through my thoughts and actions."

"I am so happy to see myself as an entrepreneur of [your dream company name], generating massive income regularly."

You need not stick to these; I suggest writing your affirmations that align with your aspirations in any area of your life. Affirmations help you visualise and believe in statements that uplift your life. **When you connect them with your career goals, they act as a silent force that pushes you forward**. Remember—affirmations work best when done regularly, consistently, and with sincerity.

---

*If you're new to this practice or wish to explore it further, consider doing so under the guidance of a **trusted mentor, guru, or mental wellness expert** of your choice. This ensures your affirmations stay aligned with your goals and emotional well-being.*

Physical Activity:

Our productivity doesn't just depend on skills or time management—it also heavily relies on our **physical fitness**. I've experienced this firsthand. There were days when I skipped any form of physical exercise, and on those days, I often felt **low on energy** and struggled to **concentrate**. Sometimes, I even felt sleepy in the middle of doing critical tasks—something that bothered me.

After reflecting on it, I realised the root cause was simple: **lack of physical movement**. Once I made that connection, I became an action taker. I started incorporating **yoga** into my routine. Soon, I noticed a noticeable improvement in my energy, focus, and overall productivity.

Physical activity became my fuel, not just for the body, but also for the mind. It becomes easier to maintain **focus, clarity, and concentration** throughout the day when we engage in physical activities. Some may think it's not easy, and they procrastinate. Embracing **physical activity as a part of our daily routine** is not a daunting task. We need a mindset shift by realising the benefits of exercise. It's a simple, achievable goal. Whether through yoga, walking, a guided workout, simple stretches, or even just dancing to your favourite music, you have the power to move your body and enhance your productivity.

Why is this so powerful? When we move, our body releases **endorphins**, the hormones that make us feel good. These not only **boost our mood** but also **calm our minds** and help in **reducing stress**. And once your mind is calm and your body is energised, productivity flows naturally.

Many experts, including *Dr. John Ratey* in his book *Spark*, highlight that movement isn't just good for the body—it's one of the simplest and most effective ways to support mental clarity and emotional balance.

What I've personally noticed is this: whenever I go for a simple 20–30-minute walk or attend a yoga session, I feel entirely energetic, even after finishing a full day of office work. It's like a natural energy booster. The type of movement and the results may vary from person to person, depending on their choice. Some may prefer walking, while others enjoy cycling; some feel better after yoga or a gym workout. But the main idea is simple: **If you want to make your day productive, physical movement adds energy to it.** It doesn't have to be intense. It just has to be **consistent**. A bit of physical activity clears your mind, lifts your mood, and brings back that spark in your body. Your choice matters.

Here are a few things to keep in mind: If you're a beginner, consider reaching out to a coach or certified practitioner who can guide you based on your body type and needs.

Additionally, even if you are not a beginner, but have a medical condition, please consult your doctor before engaging in any physical activity. Your safety is our top priority, and we want you to feel secure in your journey towards improved productivity and well-being.

Plan Your Day:

Plan your tasks and goals for a few minutes. Having a clear plan helps you stay focused and organised throughout the day.

Develop a Learning Habit:

Read, Listen, or Watch Educational Content: Continuous learning keeps your mind engaged and can inspire new ideas. Set aside time each day to read a book or listen to a podcast, Udemy, or Coursera videos related to your field or interests. You can also read self-help books. My preferred time for learning is **5:30 a.m.**

Set Learning Goals: Establish specific goals for what you want to learn. We discussed setting goals in earlier chapters; kindly refer there.

Incorporate Mindfulness and Manage Your Stress:

Incorporate mindfulness and guided meditation as part of your routine. Refer Chapter 3.3.4 for definitions, references details about Mindfulness. For guided meditation, contact experts in your vicinity or online whichever works for you.

Take Regular Breaks: From my own experience, I've realised that continuous working without breaks often leads to overwhelm, stress, and eventually, low productivity. Sitting for long hours without giving your body or mind a pause doesn't lead to fruitful results. It drains your energy and dulls your thinking.

However, you can refresh your brain and help you think more clearly and creatively. It's one of the simplest yet most powerful ways to boost your productivity. I've often heard people say, *"Work smart, not just hard."* But this smartness doesn't come by accident—it can be sharpened with timely and meaningful breaks.

Now, let's be clear: *"Taking a break means truly taking a break"*.

In my early days, I remember how we used to continue discussing work problems even during our breaks. We thought we were being efficient, but in reality, we were accelerating burnout. That kind of break isn't a break at all— it's just extending work into your recharge time. So, during breaks, make a conscious decision to disconnect from work. If possible, listen to some music, close your eyes and relax, or even take a quick nap if your environment allows. These small acts can re-energise your mind and body, making you ready for the next stretch of focused work.

Remember, productivity isn't just about pushing harder—*it's about recovering smarter.*

Many experts also support this. As *Jim Loehr* and *Tony Schwartz* explain in their book *The Power of Full Engagement(2005)*, it is not time, but energy, that plays the most vital role in sustaining high performance and personal renewal. They emphasise the importance of breaks and recovery in staying productive, focused, and emotionally balanced throughout the day.

End Your Day with Reflection:

Reflect on Your Day: Spend a few minutes each evening or night reviewing what went well and what could be improved. Reflecting on your previous actions helps you learn from your experiences and adjust your approach.

13.2 Establishing Routines for Enhanced Productivity and Work-Life Balance

Effective routines can help you manage your time better, increase productivity, and maintain a healthy work-life balance. The following section will discuss how to cultivate productivity and work-life balance.

a) Create a Structured Daily Schedule:

Set Work Hours:

This is quite challenging for our software professionals. But believe me, this is possible at least 95%, if not 100%. While working in USA, I observed that many highly productive people typically spent about nine hours working in the office, with a few exceptions. If you plan it, it's possible. It is more important to develop "laser" focus during your work time without any distractions, avoid gossip, rumours, teasing or mocking colleagues, complaining, which might distract your mind as well as productive hours. Engage in meetings only if they are relevant to you. Setting work hours helps you maintain a clear boundary between work and personal time.

Prioritise Your Tasks:

Use a task/to-do list or planner to prioritize your daily tasks. Focus on completing high-priority tasks first and tackle less critical tasks later in the day. Waking up early in the morning, exercising for 30 – 40 minutes, spending an hour on continuous learning, getting ready, offering regular prayers, having breakfast(please never miss this), dropping your spouse to the office and kids to school, giving your 100% effort with laser focus to your office work, spend quality time with family in the evening, completing leftover work if you are working across cross geographical teams(Don't spend too much here, get enough data to continue your work next day. If it takes a long time during the night, adjust your next day accordingly but don't miss even single task you planned).

Implement Time-Blocking Techniques:

Block Time for Specific Tasks: I often hear people say, *"I don't have time to read, build new skills, or even work out."* But the truth is, most of the time it's not about lack of time—it's about not giving it priority. When something doesn't feel urgent, we keep pushing it aside. That's where **time-blocking** helps.

Make it a habit to block time for the things that matter to you. If you want to develop a new skill, please put it on your calendar. In case you want to read, reflect, or even breathe, block a specific time for it. For example, you could plan focused work in the morning, meetings in the afternoon, and personal growth activities in the evening. This simple practice brings clarity and control to your day.

As *Cal Newport* mentions in his book *Deep Work*, **time-blocking** is one of the simplest ways to take control of your **schedule**. It also helps you **train your mind** to stay focused without getting distracted every few minutes. In the end, it's not just about doing more—it's about doing **what matters to you**.

Multitasking: As discussed in Section 3.1.2, while juggling across multiple projects may sometimes be necessary to meet business needs, focusing on one task at a time is crucial for boosting productivity and accuracy. It will also improve the quality of the work and minimise rework. Multitasking leads to frequent **context switching**, which drains mental energy, reduces focus, and increases the chances of making mistakes.

As *Cal Newport* explains in his book *Deep Work*, the human brain isn't designed for constant task-switching. Deep focus—where your attention is entirely on one task—produces far better results than shallow Multitasking.

So, manage your time wisely: prioritise tasks, block specific time slots for them, and commit your full attention to one thing at a time. Doing one thing with complete focus is always better than doing many things half-heartedly. **So if we want to boost our productivity, we need to do one thing at a time.**

Establish a Work-Life Balance Routine:

Personal life is essential for every professional, regardless of role, position, or experience level. After all, most of us work to support our families and create a meaningful life outside work. At the same time, we need our professional careers to earn, grow, and survive in this fast-moving world. **Both are deeply interconnected.** You can't ignore one and expect the other to thrive. That's why it's so important to bring a healthy balance between professional work and personal life.

Here are a few simple and practical strategies to help maintain that balance:

Set Boundaries:

Establish clear boundaries between work and personal life. Minimise checking work emails or taking calls outside your designated work hours (of course, with some exceptions) *(Newport, 2016)*. For more details, refer to the "Set Hour" section of "**Create a Structured Daily Schedule:**" above.

Schedule Time for Personal Life:

Just like we block time for every activity in our professional life, our personal life also deserves its own space on the calendar. Some people ignore and often say, "There's no time for exercise, family, or prayer," but the truth is—we haven't *scheduled* that time. Whether it's a refreshing morning workout, quality moments with family, reading a book, or quiet spiritual reflection, these activities fuel our energy and emotional balance.

Making time for what we love isn't a luxury—it's a necessity. Research supports this too—engaging in enjoyable activities significantly reduces stress and promotes overall well-being *(Pressman et al., 2009)*. When you care for your personal life with intention, you show up better in your professional life, too.

Maintain an Organized Workspace:

There was a time when my workspace was cluttered with work-related papers, cables, and random items scattered everywhere. Who likes such space? I didn't feel good sitting there, but I kept ignoring the same mess and telling myself it wasn't a big deal. Often, we overlook things like this, thinking they don't matter to our work.

One day, I noticed that a few of my colleagues had beautifully arranged desks. Some had motivational quotes or calming decorations. Out of curiosity, I asked one of them—someone I respect and have worked closely with—why she put so much effort into keeping her desk that way.

She smiled and said, "When my desk is clean and inspiring, I feel more motivated and positive—it changes how I work."

I took her advice and decided to give it a try.

To my surprise, something shifted. When I started keeping my workspace clean and organised, I felt calmer, more focused, and more energetic. Without even realising it, my productivity improved. That small change made a big difference in how I felt and performed.

Sometimes, it's not about changing the whole world—it's about changing the small space right in front of you.

This experience aligns with the ideas *James Clear* shares in *Atomic Habits*. He explains how small changes in our environment—like keeping a tidy, motivating workspace—can have a powerful impact on our habits, focus, and productivity.

13.3 Tools and Strategies for Maintaining Effective Habits

Maintaining productive habits and routines requires consistency and using the right tools. In the previous chapter, we discussed a few tools for achieving goals. But here discuss tools and effective strategies for habit tracking:

Use Habit-Tracking Apps:

Track Your Progress: Apps like Habitica, Streaks, or HabitBull can help you stay consistent by tracking your daily habits. These apps often provide reminders and visual dashboards to show your progress, which can be surprisingly motivating. As James Clear explains in *Atomic Habits*, even small visual cues or rewards—like streak counters—can reinforce habit formation over time (Clear, 2018). Just make sure you enter your data honestly and daily. Remember, you are your boss.

Set Reminders: Use app reminders to prompt you to complete specific tasks. It prevents you from forgetting necessary steps and helps embed new behaviours into your daily rhythm. Setting reminders is a simple yet effective cue to nudge your brain toward consistency.

Leverage Task Management Tools:

Create Task Lists and Planners: Tools like Todoist, Microsoft To Do, or Google Calendar help you organise and prioritise tasks effectively. The moment you write something down, it frees mental spaces, so that you no longer need to think about that task again. The app will remind you when you need to accomplish that. *David Allen*, in *Getting Things Done*, emphasises how externalising your tasks reduces mental clutter and increases clarity (Allen, 2001).

Plan Your Week: Spend time planning your weekly tasks and goals. Having a clear weekly plan helps you stay organised and focused.

Build Accountability:

Share Your Goals: You can be your accountability partner, but it's even more effective if you have a friend, family member, or colleague who shares your goals. Having someone hold you accountable is better, which can boost your commitment to your habits. Even if you miss or want to miss some days, your partner can remind you about your goals. As *James Clear* highlights in *Atomic Habits*, the support and encouragement from others can make it easier to keep going and maintain good habits.

Join a Support Group: Find or form a group that shares your values or goals—whether it's fitness, learning, or career growth. The motivation you get from like-minded individuals is incredible. When you're surrounded by people moving in the same direction, it becomes easier to stay focused, consistent, and motivated.

Adjust and Adapt:

We also discussed this in the previous chapter in the context of productivity tasks. The same principles apply to habits as well.

Be Flexible: Recognise that routines and habits may need adjustments over time. Life isn't static, and neither are we. We should be flexible enough to modify our approach based on what works best for us. *James Clear*, in *Atomic Habits*, emphasises that habits are systems that evolve, and adjusting them is part of sustaining them.

Celebrate Small Wins: Acknowledging and celebrating even minor progress helps you stay motivated and reinforces a positive attitude. These little victories build momentum. As **Clear** points out, small, consistent steps create lasting change.

Evaluate and Reflect:

Regularly Review Your Habits: Periodically evaluate your habits and routines to assess their effectiveness. Identify what's working well and where improvements are needed. Use a journal to reflect on patterns and take corrective actions based on those insights. According to *Baumeister and Vohs (2007)*, self-monitoring is a foundational strategy for effective self-regulation, goal achievement, and long-term behaviour change.

Adjustments: Based on your reflection, tweak your routines. Continuous, minor improvements keep you aligned with your bigger vision.

Summary

This chapter focuses on building productive habits and routines to navigate challenges in the software industry effectively. By intentionally incorporating these practices, professionals can nurture a positive mindset, boost productivity, and achieve a harmonious work-life balance.

Some of the key strategies include:

- **Fostering positive habits**, such as waking up early.

- **Engaging in physical exercise** to stay energised.

- **Practising gratitude** fosters optimism.

- **Using affirmations** to build confidence.

- **Adopting mindfulness techniques** for clarity and focus.

Incorporating daily exercises, planning, and consistent learning into routines promotes mental clarity and supports ongoing growth. Structured approaches like time-blocking and prioritising tasks further enhance focus and efficiency, empowering professionals to thrive in their roles.

Effective routines are essential for balancing work and personal life. This involves setting clear boundaries, scheduling time for relaxation and hobbies, and maintaining an organised workspace to minimise distractions and encourage creativity.

The chapter also highlights the value of reflection and self-improvement. Ending each day by reviewing achievements and lessons learned helps professionals grow and adapt continually. By embedding these habits into daily life, individuals can build resilience, find fulfilment, and pave the way for long-term success—programming success and balance into their routines like a well-designed algorithm.

Your Journey Ahead: Putting It All Together

Step 1: Define Your Vision

- Clarify your personal, professional, and technical success goals.

- Use visualization, gratitude, and affirmations to reinforce your vision.

Step 2: Cultivate the Right Mindset

- Embrace challenges as opportunities to learn and grow.

- Build resilience by reframing failures as stepping stones.

- Increase self-awareness to overcome mental blocks.

Step 3: Set and Track Goals

- Define SMART goals for short and long terms.

- Review and adjust your goals regularly.

- Use tools like to-do lists or Kanban boards to track progress.

Step 4: Commit to Continuous Learning

- Stay updated on new technologies and methodologies.

- Learn through books, courses, and hands-on projects.

- Reflect on learning to deepen understanding.

Step 5: Foster Creativity and Problem-Solving

- Engage with inspiring resources and diverse ideas.

- Apply creative techniques such as mind mapping or design thinking.

Step 6: Enhance Collaboration and Influence

- Communicate clearly and respectfully with colleagues.

- Support your team by sharing knowledge and ideas.

- Build trust by being dependable and open to feedback.

Step 7: Use Feedback and Self-Reflection

- Actively seek constructive feedback.

- Reflect on your strengths and areas for growth.

- Implement changes based on insights gained.

Step 8: Adapt to Industry Changes

- Monitor tech trends and be ready to reskill.

- Keep your skill set versatile to embrace new opportunities.

Step 9: Build and Nurture Your Network

- Connect meaningfully with mentors, peers, and professionals.

- Participate in meetups, webinars, and tech communities.

- Collaborate and contribute value to your network.

Step 10: Balance Passion and Well-Being

- Align your work with your values and passions.

- Prioritize physical, emotional, and mental health.

- Recharge through hobbies and rest to sustain creativity.

Step 11: Celebrate Your Success

- Acknowledge milestones and progress.

- Share achievements to inspire yourself and others.

- Use success as motivation for continuous growth.

Step 12: Apply the Ritual Algorithm

- **Plan:** Set clear daily or weekly intentions.

- **Act:** Execute with focus and commitment.

- **Reflect:** Review outcomes and lessons.

- **Iterate:** Adjust plans based on feedback and reflection.

The Concluding Message of the Success Algorithm

Unleashing your potential in the software world goes beyond technical expertise. It's about adopting a growth mindset, staying resilient, and committing to continuous learning. This book highlights the importance of seeing challenges as growth opportunities, embracing feedback as a tool for improvement, and developing resilience in the face of setbacks.

Your success algorithm blends creativity, strategic thinking, and the ability to adapt to the ever-changing software landscape. Celebrating milestones and reflecting on achievements is crucial for maintaining motivation, while collaboration and mentorship magnify your impact, enabling you to reach new heights.

The success algorithm is a harmonious fusion of creativity, strategic insight, and adaptability that helps you thrive in the fast-paced software world. Embracing challenges and celebrating milestones ensures sustained motivation, while collaboration and mentorship empower you to expand your influence and achieve greater success.

Though this book doesn't cover every concept, I've intentionally focused on what's most essential. One critical skill for software professionals—*leadership*—will be explored in my upcoming book(s).

Stay tuned...

– Sreenath Natarajan
Software Professional

Summary of Key Revisions

1. **Emotional Refinement**

   - Motivation and "Why Read This Book" sections rewritten with a deeper emotional connection to engage readers more meaningfully.

2. **Structural Enhancements**

   - Introduction and Chapter 1 merged into a new opening chapter titled **"Decoding Success Algorithm."**

   - Chapter and subchapter numbering updated to align with international publishing standards.

   - **About the Author** moved to the end and made more generic by removing company-specific references.

3. **Content Expansion**

   - Added new sections on **fear of failure, imposter syndrome, career stagnation, interview tips**, and **Go language interview preparation**.

   - Expanded existing topics like **affirmations, physical activity, time blocking**, and **productivity at work** with both personal insights and practical guidance.

4. **Voice and Tone Enhancements**

   - Infused personal commentary and authentic storytelling to make the content more relatable.

- Rewrote several sections in my own tone to improve clarity and engagement.

5. **Visual Maturity & Formatting**

   - Removed several diagrams to present a more professional and mature tone.

   - Replaced diagrams with **clear textual explanations** and added **mind maps** where relevant.

6. **Credibility Improvements**

   - Provided **clear definitions** of core concepts like the **Success Algorithm**.

   - Added relevant **citations and references** both chapter-wise and in a dedicated **"References and Further Reading"** section.

7. **Compliance and Final Additions**

   - Included a **disclaimer** section.

   - Updated **bibliography** to include all sources that inspired or supported the content.

   - Rewrote and refined the final sections to improve flow and coherence.

References and Further Reading

Decoding Success Algorithm

- **Ashe, A. (n.d.).** "Success is a journey, not a destination..." [Quote widely attributed; original source not confirmed].

- **Dweck, C. S. (2006).** *Mindset: The new psychology of success.* Random House. Refer this book *For a deeper understanding of the mindset concept. Only essential ideas are covered in this book.*

- **Nightingale, E. (1956).** *The strangest secret.* Nightingale-Conant.

- **Ziglar, Z. (1975).** *See you at the top.* Pelican Publishing.

- **The Open Group. (2022).** *TOGAF® standard, version 9.2.* https://pubs.opengroup.org

Chapter 1: Code Your Mindset: Diagnosing Current Limitations

- **Beck, A. T. (1976).** *Cognitive therapy and the emotional disorders.* International Universities Press.

- **Doran, G. T. (1981).** There's a S.M.A.R.T. way to write management's goals and objectives. *Management Review, 70*(11), 35–36.

- **Buzan, T. (1996).** *The mind map book: Unlock your creativity, boost your memory, change your life.* BBC Books.

- **Covey, S. R. (1989).** *The 7 habits of highly effective people: Powerful lessons in personal change.* Free Press.

- **Doerr, J. (2018).** *Measure what matters: How Google, Bono, and the Gates Foundation rock the world with OKRs.* Portfolio.

- **Goleman, D. (1995).** *Emotional intelligence: Why it can matter more than IQ.* Bantam Books.

- **Robbins, T. (2001).** *Awaken the giant within: How to take immediate control of your mental, emotional, physical and financial destiny!.* Free Press.

- **Seligman, M. E. P. (1975).** *Helplessness: On depression, development, and death.* W.H. Freeman.

- **The Agile Manifesto. (2001).** *Manifesto for agile software development.* https://agilemanifesto.org

- **Upanishads. (n.d.).** *Brhadaranyaka Upanishad* (Trans. Swami Madhavananda). Advaita Ashrama.

Chapter 2: Refactoring Your Thinking: Upgrading to a Growth Mindset

- **Brhadaranyaka Upanishad. (n.d.).** Chapter 1, verse 3.28. [Ancient Sanskrit scripture].

- **Cirillo, F. (2018).** *The pomodoro technique: The life-changing time-management system.* Random House.

- **Johnson, S. (1998).** *Who moved my cheese? An A-mazing way to deal with change in your work and in your life.* G.P. Putnam's Sons.

- **Kabat-Zinn, J. (1990).** *Full catastrophe living: Using the wisdom of your body and mind to face stress, pain, and illness.* Dell Publishing.

Chapter 3: Agile Goal Setting: Navigating Your Software Career

- **Google. (2009).** Go programming language. https://golang.org

- **Python Software Foundation. (2001).** The Python programming language. https://www.python.org

- **Beck, K., Beedle, M., van Bennekum, A., Cockburn, A., Cunningham, W., Fowler, M., … Thomas, D. (2001).** Manifesto for agile software development. https://agilemanifesto.org

- **Kanban and Scrum methodologies. (n.d.).** Agile frameworks overview. https://scrumguides.org

- **Atlassian. (n.d.).** JIRA software. https://www.atlassian.com/software/jira

- The Open Group. (n.d.). TOGAF® standard. https://www.opengroup.org/togaf

Chapter 4: Debugging Challenges: Cultivating Resilience

- **Amabile, T. M., & Kramer, S. J. (2011).** *The progress principle: Using small wins to ignite joy, engagement, and creativity at work.* Harvard Business Review Press.

- **Clance, P. R., & Imes, S. A. (1978).** The imposter phenomenon in high achieving women: Dynamics and therapeutic intervention. *Psychotherapy: Theory, Research & Practice, 15*(3), 241–247.

- **Ellis, A. (1994).** *A guide to rational living* (3rd ed.). Wilshire Book Company.

- **Mental Health America. (2025, February 27).** What is emotional intelligence and how does it apply to the workplace? https://www.mhanational.org/learning-hub/what-is-emotional-intelligence-and-how-does-it-apply-to-the-workplace

- **Neff, K. (2011).** *Self-compassion: The proven power of being kind to yourself.* William Morrow.

- **Neff, K., & Germer, C. (2013).** *The mindful self-compassion workbook: A proven way to accept yourself, build inner strength, and thrive.* Guilford Press.

- **Newport, C. (2016).** *Deep work: Rules for focused success in a distracted world.* Grand Central Publishing.

- **The Bhagavad Gita. (n.d.).** Chapter 6, verse 5. (Various translations).

Chapter 5: The Web of Opportunity: Interlacing Connections for Career Advancement

- **Keller, H. (1903).** *Optimism: An essay.* Thomas Y. Crowell & Co.

- **Covey, S. R. (1989).** *The 7 habits of highly effective people: Powerful lessons in personal change.* Free Press.

- **LinkedIn Corporation. (n.d.).** https://www.linkedin.com

- **GitHub, Inc. (n.d.).** https://github.com

- **Stack Exchange, Inc. (n.d.).** Stack Overflow. https://stackoverflow.com

- **Google LLC. (n.d.).** Google Groups. https://groups.google.com

- **RFC Editor / IETF. (n.d.).** Request for comments (RFC) series. https://www.rfc-editor.org

Chapter 6: The Learning River: Flowing with Change in the Tech Landscape

- **Bhagavad Gita. (n.d.).** Chapter 4, verse 38. [Ancient Indian scripture].

- **Luft, J., & Ingham, H. (1955).** The Johari window model. [Psychological framework].

- **AWS re:Invent. (n.d.).** https://reinvent.awsevents.com

- **Google I/O. (n.d.).** https://io.google

- **Microsoft Build. (n.d.).** https://build.microsoft.com

- **Udemy. (n.d.).** https://www.udemy.com

- **Coursera. (n.d.).** https://www.coursera.org

- **LinkedIn Learning. (n.d.).** https://www.linkedin.com/learning

- **Udacity. (n.d.).** https://www.udacity.com

- **edX. (n.d.).** https://www.edx.org

- **YouTube. (n.d.).** https://www.youtube.com

- **Reddit. (n.d.).** https://www.reddit.com

Chapter 7: The Human Circuit: Powering Tech Teams with Emotional Intelligence

- **Bradberry, T., & Greaves, J. (2009).** *Emotional intelligence 2.0.* TalentSmart.

- **Edmondson, A. C. (2019).** *The fearless organization: Creating psychological safety in the workplace for learning, innovation, and growth.* Wiley.

- **García, H., & Miralles, F. (2016).** *Ikigai: The Japanese secret to a long and happy life.*

- **Stone, D., Patton, B., & Heen, S. (1999).** *Difficult conversations: How to discuss what matters most.* Penguin Books.

Chapter 8: Visionary Coding: Crafting Your Career Path

- **Byrne, R. (2006).** *The secret.* Atria Books.

- **Gawain, S. (2020).** *Creative visualization: Use the power of your imagination to create what you want in your life.* New World Library.

- **Iyengar, B. K. S. (1993).** *Light on pranayama: The yogic art of breathing.* HarperCollins.

- **Tracy, B. (2004).** *Goals!: How to get everything you want—faster than you ever thought possible.* Berrett-Koehler Publishers.

- **Dr. Manjunath, M. (n.d.).** Unleashing the power of reading [Workshop reference]. Personal communication.

Chapter 9: Planting Seeds of Innovation: Cultivating Creativity and Problem-Solving Skills for Growth

- **Buzan, T. (1993).** *The mind map book: Radiant thinking.* BBC Active.

- **Osborn, A. F. (1953).** *Applied imagination: Principles and procedures of creative problem-solving.* Charles Scribner's Sons.

- **Houston, D., & Ferdowsi, A. (2007).** Dropbox. www.dropbox.com

- **Butterfield, S. (2013).** Slack. www.slack.com

- **GitHub. (n.d.).** www.github.com

- **Twitter Engineering Blog. (n.d.).** https://blog.twitter.com/engineering

- **Netflix Tech Blog. (n.d.).** https://netflixtechblog.com

- **Boardmix. (n.d.).** https://boardmix.com

Chapter 10: Building the Bridge to Success: Tracking Milestones and Metrics

- **Collier, R. (n.d.).** Success is the sum of small efforts, repeated day in and day out. Goodreads. https://www.goodreads.com/quotes/30653

- **Gallo, A. (2011).** Where will you be in five years? *Harvard Business Review.* https://hbr.org/2011/03/where-will-you-be-in-five-year

- **Agile Alliance. (n.d.).** Agile retrospectives & continuous improvement. https://www.agilealliance.org

- **Atlassian JIRA. (n.d.).** https://www.atlassian.com/software/jira

- **Trello. (n.d.).** https://trello.com

- **Asana. (n.d.).** https://asana.com

- **Todoist. (n.d.).** https://todoist.com

- **Notion. (n.d.).** https://www.notion.so

- **Evernote. (n.d.).** https://evernote.com

- **Parmenter, D. (2015).** *Key performance indicators: Developing, implementing, and using winning KPIs* (3rd ed.). Wiley.

Chapter 11: Harvesting the Fruits of Success: The Role of Recognition in the Software World

- **Pink, D. H. (2009).** *Drive: The surprising truth about what motivates us.* Riverhead Books.

- **Amabile, T. M., & Kramer, S. J. (2011).** *The progress principle: Using small wins to ignite joy, engagement, and creativity at work.* Harvard Business Review Press.

- **Duckworth, A. (2016).** *Grit: The power of passion and perseverance.* Scribner.

- **Clear, J. (2018).** *Atomic habits: An easy & proven way to build good habits & break bad ones.* Avery.

- **Allen, D. (2001).** *Getting things done: The art of stress-free productivity.* Penguin Books.

- **Drucker, P. F. (1967).** *The effective executive: The definitive guide to getting the right things done.* HarperBusiness.

- **Brown, B. (2018).** *Dare to lead: Brave work. Tough conversations. Whole hearts.* Random House.

Chapter 12: Navigating Career Transitions and Growth Opportunities

- **Kolb, D. A. (1984).** *Experiential learning: Experience as the source of learning and development.* Prentice-Hall.

- **American Psychological Association. (2022).** Resilience. https://www.apa.org/topics/resilience

- **Chamorro-Premuzic, T., & Yearsley, A. (2017).** The best job on paper isn't always the right one. *Harvard Business Review.*

- **Cross, R., & Thomas, R. J. (2011).** Building smart networks. *Harvard Business Review.*

- **LinkedIn Learning. (n.d.).** Career development and transition planning. https://www.linkedin.com/learning

- **Indeed Career Guide. (n.d.).** How to research a company before applying. https://www.indeed.com/career-advice/interviewing/how-to-research-company-before-interview

- **World Economic Forum. (2023).** The future of jobs report. https://www.weforum.org/reports/the-future-of-jobs-report-2023

Chapter 13: The Ritual Algorithm: Programming Success into Your Life

- **Clear, J. (2018).** *Atomic habits: An easy & proven way to build good habits & break bad ones.* Avery.

- **Newport, C. (2016).** *Deep work: Rules for focused success in a distracted world.* Grand Central Publishing.

- **Loehr, J., & Schwartz, T. (2005).** *The power of full engagement: Managing energy, not time, is the key to high performance and personal renewal.* Free Press.

- **Ratey, J. J. (2008).** *Spark: The revolutionary new science of exercise and the brain.* Little, Brown Spark.

- **Allen, D. (2001).** *Getting things done: The art of stress-free productivity.* Penguin.

Tools & Apps

- **Habitica. (n.d.).** https://habitica.com

- **Streaks. (n.d.).** https://streaksapp.com

- **HabitBull. (n.d.).** https://www.habitbull.com

- **Todoist. (n.d.).** https://todoist.com

- **Google Calendar. (n.d.).** https://calendar.google.com

- **Microsoft To Do. (n.d.).** https://todo.microsoft.com

Learning Platforms

- **Coursera. (n.d.).** https://www.coursera.org

- **Udemy. (n.d.).** https://www.udemy.com

Mindfulness & Meditation

- **Headspace. (n.d.).** https://www.headspace.com

- **Insight Timer. (n.d.).** https://insighttimer.com

- **UMass Center for Mindfulness (MBSR).** (n.d.). https://www.umassmed.edu/cfm

Disclaimer

The Success Algorithm: Unleashing Your Full Potential in the Software World" is a unique work shaped by the author's professional experiences, reflections, and insights within the software domain. It is intended purely for educational, motivational, and informational use.

All trademarks, product names, logos, and platform references (e.g., LinkedIn, GitHub, Stack Overflow, Google Groups) belong to their respective owners. Their mention in this book serves only illustrative or educational purposes, and does not imply any association, sponsorship, or endorsement.

The frameworks, analogies, and perspectives shared are drawn from the author's understanding and interpretations of broadly accepted principles in career growth, leadership, and software development. Any resemblance to existing theories or content is coincidental or due to shared universal ideas. To the best of the author's knowledge, all references have been acknowledged. Any unintentional oversight will be addressed in future updates upon notification.

Certain case studies, examples, and personal names have been altered or anonymized to ensure privacy. Any similarities to actual individuals, businesses, or real events are unintentional unless clearly stated otherwise.

This book is not a substitute for professional advice—legal, medical, financial, psychological, or career-related. Readers are advised to consult qualified professionals for guidance tailored to their needs. *The author and publisher shall not be held liable for any outcomes resulting from actions taken based on this book's content.* Outcomes may differ based on individual efforts, timing, and circumstances.

This work is offered as a general guide and does not replace expert input or contextual analysis. It is the responsibility of the reader to interpret the content and comply with local regulations or professional standards.

About Author

Sreenath Natarajan is a seasoned software professional with extensive experience in building robust software systems across the ever-evolving and dynamic technical landscape. With a strong academic background with a Bachelor's degree in Engineering from a reputable college, he developed a deep passion for learning—not just for himself, but to uplift and support those around him.

Over the years, Sreenath has worked on cutting-edge projects spanning mobile applications, network products, containerized systems, and resilient, high-availability architectures. His solid foundation in software development led him to a crucial realization: **technical, managerial, or even marketing skills alone are not enough to truly thrive**. It's the **mindset** that plays a mammoth role in navigating challenges and achieving lasting success in the software world.

Throughout his professional journey, he has played key roles in designing, coding, and optimizing business-critical applications tailored to real organizational needs. What drives him is a strong commitment to continuous learning, powered by a growth mindset. He draws inspiration from diverse areas—software engineering, personal growth, and spiritual wisdom—all of which energize his career path and shape his personal evolution.

As a mentor and leader, Sreenath has built and guided high-performing teams, consistently encouraging collaboration and helping others realize their full potential. His passion for mentorship has empowered many aspiring professionals to grow—not just as skilled engineers, but as future leaders as well.

Beyond software, Sreenath enjoys playing chess and cricket—activities that sharpen his strategic thinking and reinforce his love for teamwork. He is also deeply passionate about public speaking and content creation, using these platforms to share insights on technology, career development, and mindful living.

With *The Success Algorithm*, Sreenath brings together his hands-on experiences, evolving mindset, and grounded values to inspire software professionals to overcome obstacles, adapt with confidence, and thrive in the ever-changing world of technology.